CW00548298

CHINA TO CHITRAL

H. W. TILMAN

(1) The water front, Shanghai—a placid scene which gives no hint of
the tumult of traffic on the Bund from which the picture was taken

CHINA TO CHITRAL

H. W. TILMAN

TILMAN

First published 1951 by Cambridge University Press
This edition published 2016 by Tilman Books
www.tilmanbooks.com
a joint venture by
Lodestar Books www.lodestarbooks.com
and Vertebrate Publishing www.v-publishing.co.uk

Original text copyright © Simon Heyworth Davis 1951
Additional material copyright © the contributors 2016

Cover design by Jane Beagley
Vertebrate Graphics Ltd. www.v-graphics.co.uk

Lodestar Books has asserted their right
to be identified as the Editor of this Work

Series editor Dick Wynne
Series researcher Bob Comlay

The publisher has made reasonable effort to locate
the holders of copyright in the illustrations in this book,
and will be pleased to hear from them regarding
correct attribution in future editions

All rights reserved

A CIP catalogue record for this book
is available from the British Library

ISBN 978-1-909461-34-5

Typeset in Baskerville from Storm Type Foundry
Printed and bound by Pulsio, Bulgaria
All papers used by Tilman Books are sourced responsibly

Contents

Photographs

Maps

Foreword

Tony Howard

IT'S STRANGE HOW THINGS HAPPEN: whilst walking and climbing for the first time in years in Cwm Mynach in the Rhinog Hills, a pretty place hidden high above the Mawddach Estuary in mid-Wales, I remembered that Bill Tilman used to live close by and imagined him enjoying this quiet mountain valley. Then on our way home I had an email from Vertebrate asking if I would like to write the Foreword to this reprint of his book of mountain exploration and travel from China to Chitral. I recalled he had invited me to his cottage one evening for a drink and a chat after I had been lecturing on the Troll Wall in nearby Barmouth. How could I refuse? He has long been one of my heroes, an incomparable mountaineer, sailor and traveller, in search of the unknown, and the enviable and inevitable adventures that entails.

His explorations and climbs with Eric Shipton (I won't call them 'expeditions' since both were aficionados of going small and light, or 'alpine style' as it's now known) are the stuff of legend, as are his voyages in *Mischief* and subsequent pilot cutters. He preferred to travel simply with the minimum of equipment and food, and in the company of one or two close companions, relying on, and usually enjoying, the hospitality of local people rather than being burdened with baggage he felt was superfluous. Travelling light in this way, as he says, 'doesn't always make for easy travel, but more often than not it makes for interesting travel'. I agree wholeheartedly, it's definitely the way to go.

As with any eternally inquisitive explorer he has 'a rooted objection to following the beaten track' and rightly says, 'By risking nothing, nothing can be gained', adding, 'On the whole I think that Romance in travel is inseparable from an element of risk'. His reference to Romance with a capital R refers here to the feeling of mystery, excitement, and remoteness from everyday life that being in uncharted areas brings, rather than its more common amorous connotation. Tilman was a single man with a reputation as a misogynist though I suspect his concerns regarding women were more to do with the marital ties and obligations that would keep him from his travels. He would have liked Steinbeck's 'A journey is like marriage. The certain way to be wrong is to think you control it'. He himself quotes one of Sancho Panza's witticisms from *Don Quixote* that, 'A wife's counsel is bad but he who will not take it is mad'—but that doesn't stop him noting that, 'All the Aqsu girls were graceful and many of them comely'.

He surprised me in his Preface with a disparaging comment more true now than then. He says, typically tongue in cheek, 'Since nowadays so few people can be bothered to read, the text is brief, but the pictures numerous'. But fine and fascinating the pictures are. And the text is not that brief though an easy read that speeds you on a wonderful journey of discovery. Virtually every sentence is a gem of observation concerning the mountains he climbed (and sometimes didn't) and the little known lands, peoples, customs and cultures through which he travelled, 'whose very remoteness forms a deadly lure'. With which comment I couldn't agree more, though perhaps I should be careful about using the word 'travel' too often; he advises us that simply to be a passenger on any form of motorised transport is insufficient, a 'traveller must exert himself and move slowly'. Indeed!

He also surprised me with his humour as, though he was both amiable and chatty when I met him, he has a reputation for being an unsociable and reticent man of few words and friends. This book shows another side with his witty comments and often self-deprecating humour permeating the pages. If you can read his descriptions of travel, its vicissitudes, the people he meets along the way and the frequently alien food (and sometimes the over abundance or total lack of it) without at least smiling or more likely laughing out loud, I'd be surprised. It's a travel yarn at its best, taking the reader through a little known and sometimes untravelled world now fast vanishing if not already gone, told by an erudite raconteur able to laugh at life regardless of circumstances, and all the more inspirational for it.

Tony Howard
October 2015

Preface

COMPARATIVELY FEW TRAVELLERS have visited Chinese Turkestan; which is perhaps just as well because, of those fortunate few, not many have refrained from writing a book. Much has been written about the deserts, the buried cities, and the living oases, but less about its more serious aspect as a rich field for mountaineers. True, the great Central Asian traveller and explorer Sven Hedin took time off from serious exploration to make a light-hearted attempt on Muztagh Ata (*Through Asia*, vol. 1) but he soon returned to the recording of astronomical observations and thermometer readings at lower levels. My theme is mountains, unsullied by science and alleviated with Chinese brandy.

Since nowadays so few people can be bothered to read, the text is brief but the pictures numerous.

Once more I am indebted to Dr R. J. Perring for much helpful criticism and advice.

H.W.T.
Barmouth
April 1950

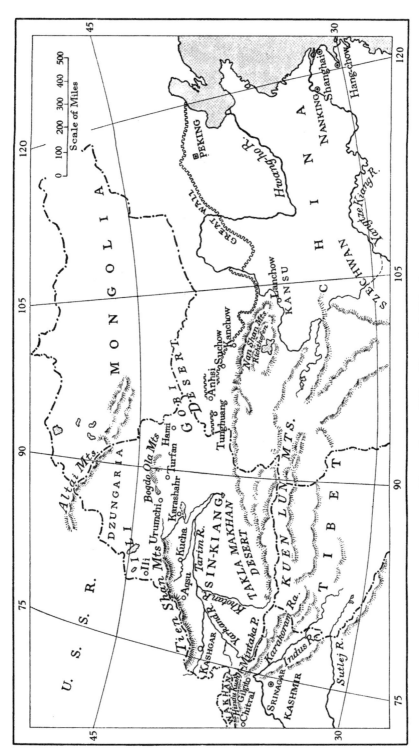

Map 1: General Map, Shanghai-Chitral

CHAPTER I

TRAVELLER OR PASSENGER?

———————◆———————

'BETTER FIFTY YEARS OF EUROPE than a cycle of Cathay' is a sentiment that might well be endorsed by a man who has seen no more of China than, say, Shanghai. But within the borders of Cathay is Chinese Turkestan, and for my part, having seen only a little of that fascinating country in 1947, I did not mind how soon or how often I saw it again. There can be no part of Asia, or indeed of any continent, which exerts a more powerful attraction on either the mountaineer, the geographer, the archaeologist, or any man who travels merely 'for to admire an' for to see'.

In the first place its very remoteness forms a deadly lure for the ambitious traveller. Some of the peaks and valleys of the Himalaya are also remote, but their appeal is mainly to the mountaineer. In time even he may become satiated with rocks, snow, and glaciers, and when he reluctantly or, perhaps, gladly descends to grass, forest, and villages, he finds with few exceptions that the villages are only the slightly squalid homes of a cheerful but uninteresting people without history, arts, or even trade. I have had many happy and amusing hours and enjoyed much hospitality in Himalayan villages and I think that, although one must be grateful to and respect those contented, hard-working, penurious folk, their villages are not one of the main attractions. They are merely incidents on the route, depots for the recruiting of porters, sources of food, or perhaps places where beer is brewed.

In Chinese Turkestan, or Sinkiang, the lures are many. Where else is there such a startling and satisfying mixture of desert and mountain, of Moslem and Buddhist, of settled folk and nomad? where the bread and melons of the one are rivalled by the cream, yoghourt, and kumis of the other; and all these found in a country of historic fame, a country which itself has undergone but little change and which was once the link between the great civilizations of China on the one hand, and of India, Persia, or even Europe, on the other. There are spacious deserts elsewhere; some also holding the buried secrets of past civilizations; but nowhere else is there such a desert fringed with rich and teeming oases, shut in on three sides by vast snow ranges whose glacier streams nourish the oases and upon whose slopes yaks and camels graze side by side; where in their felt yorts Kirghiz and Kazak live much as they did in the days of Gengiz Khan, except that now they no longer take a hand in the devastation of Europe.

Just as it is a good thing to have a friend at court, so it is good to have a friend in a remote country, especially when it is hedged about by political barriers under which the meek must crawl. In 1948 my friend Mr E. E. Shipton, in the post of Consul General Kashgar, was still spreading his beneficent rays over Kashgaria, touching sometimes distant Dzungaria, or at least Urumchi which lies on its outskirts. Within easy reach of this place Urumchi, the capital of Sinkiang, there is a mountain called Bogdo Ola upon which Shipton had long meditated assault, and it was in order to aid and abet him in this attempt that in May of that year I turned up at Shanghai.

To reach Central Asia by way of Shanghai may seem a Chestertonian approach, reminiscent of 'the night we went to Birmingham by way of Beachy Head'; but by sinking one's pride and opening one's purse wide enough to take advantage of air travel, such an indirect approach takes no longer than the ordinary routes. From England the usual way to Sinkiang is from India, either through Kashmir to Leh and thence over the Karakoram Pass (19,000 ft.), or through Gilgit and over the Mintaka Pass (15,000 ft.), both of which routes, particularly the first, are hard on man and beast. I am not averse to hard travel, in fact in retrospect I like it, but in 1948 owing to the Kashmir dispute the first was impossible and the second doubtful. Moreover, both these routes lead to Kashgar, while Urumchi, to which Shipton had already gone, is a thousand miles further east.

Instead of saying I travelled to Shanghai by air I should prefer to say I was carried there; for it seems to me time to draw a hard and fast line between travellers and passengers before the word 'traveller' loses its romantic flavour. A journey of many thousands of miles by air and bus, such as that which I undertook to Urumchi, without the least physical effort on my part and with a despicably small increase of knowledge as a result, can hardly be called travelling. To my mind two

(2) Looking down from the walls at Kanchow across the modern
quarter to the Hall of the Sleeping Buddha; even the modern part is
not without its willows and poplars

(3) In the old quarter of Kanchow, a house with curling projecting
roof of warm glazed tiles and elaborately carved eaves and
supporting brackets

distinguishing marks of a traveller are that he exerts himself and that he moves slowly. Indeed, this must be so by definition; for to travel is defined as to pass from point to point in a *deliberate* and systematic manner; while the qualification that he must exert himself was recognised by those most potent, grave, and reverend signiors who drew up our admirable licensing laws, when they defined the *bona fide* traveller (with whom we are concerned) as one entitled to call for refreshment on Sunday at public houses by having *walked* three miles.

The Chinese saying that the further one travels the less one knows must have been prescient of the air age. Nothing could be truer of air travel. It is about 10,000 miles from London to Shanghai, a journey which had it been done by sea in a small boat, overland on foot, or even by car, would have provided an education in itself, a bottomless fund of anecdote, and perhaps a final eradication of that tormenting desire for travel. Whereas when it is done by air the traveller is poorer in pocket and no richer in experience. Nor is his appetite for travel satisfied; it is merely whetted. Places like Singapore, Bangkok, and Hong Kong, which were just names to me when I started, were still names when I was dumped at Shanghai, but which now kindled in me a dangerous spark of interest.

I realised at once that I should have visited Shanghai many years earlier—a surmise which probably holds good for most parts of the inhabited globe—before the first world war, perhaps, when Englishmen and even Europeans still had 'face', and when the presence of numerous 'old China hands' made even the longest bar in the world a desirable goal. But in 1948 Shanghai (Photo 1) seemed to me a place that one could hardly leave too quickly. I suppose it was not unnatural, but there were a great many Chinese, far too many, all of them apparently in the streets at once, in cars, in pedi-cabs, and a multitude on foot.

Despite the teaching of Taoism the Chinese, at any rate in private life, are active, bustling people with an eye firmly fixed on the main chance. Not for them, 'the business of Tao which is one of day by day dealing with less and less until you arrive at inaction'. On the contrary, all of them appeared to be in trade and all those who were not serving in one or other army, tilling rice or drowning in a Yangtze flood, had assembled in Shanghai to ply their vocations. There were not enough shops or even barrows for the five million inhabitants of Shanghai, but there was plenty of pavement which could be used as business premises. Thus anyone not actually buying or selling had to walk in the street among the cars, pedi-cabs, and foot people, all of necessity going the same pace. Fruit sellers predominated; bananas were in season; and judging by the number of cast-off skins most of the five million seemed to be in favour of eating more fruit. In short, the impressions I took away were of too much noise, dirt, heat and a population badly in need of decimation—either by planning or by some less subtle means.

But to return to my thesis. The distinction between a traveller and a passenger is that the one uses travel as an end in itself while the other is merely carried as a means to an end. If I seem to disparage air travel, which is a very handy means of transport, it is partly to excuse my ignorance of China. For though I may now talk of having travelled in China, indeed even of having crossed it—being hurtled halfway in the course of one day by air and hurtled the remainder in twelve days by lorry—I am yet no sinologue. The true traveller, as I have said, must move by his own exertions, while the passenger is moved swiftly by machinery. My distinction is not a hole-proof definition, for I can conceive of circumstances in which the passenger moves so slowly as to have time to look about him, thereby qualifying as a traveller. In which category the occupants of a Chinese controlled bus must be placed is hard to say for, although they do not move so very slowly, there are other factors which come into play.

Consider for a moment a bus which I boarded in Nanking. The mere boarding of it was a bold step which few of the class derogatively described as 'passengers' would have taken, for I knew neither Chinese nor where I wanted to go. Nanking is like Euclid's definition of a line—length without breadth—for it consists of a street six miles long. The hotel in which I stayed—truthfully describable as quaint and old world—was at one extremity and I had to get myself and a suitcase to the other. Buses ran frequently and mostly under their own power, so that I concede that once inside one was technically speaking a passenger. But to get in called for some personal effort, in fact for the utmost violence, and no less was needed to get out.

Those tiresome people who constantly remind us that a pint pot holds only a pint never can have seen a Nanking bus. There, private enterprise had free play. There were no trammelling by-laws; and

(4) Kanchow, a gate leading to the modern main street; the massive walls of the gateway end in mid-air; one often sees such 'token' gateways—perhaps erected in a wide, open space—which, since they are built, must be gone through though it would be very much easier for vehicles to go round

(5) More curly roofs, certainly very like a badly pitched ridge tent; the Chinese are as fond of wall slogans as the Italians; is this one a precept of Confucius or merely 'Eat more Rice'?

evidently the conductor had a large personal stake in the success of his bus; for there was no nonsense about standing room for eight only. The capacity of the bus was limited only by the amount of compression a passenger could sustain, and yet live. And in the event, hardly by that, because the step, the bonnet, and any excrescence to which a human foot could adhere took a share of the payload. To insert oneself in the door like the thin end of a wedge was difficult, but it was enough. Fellow combatants, like so many mauls, drove one right home, and having thus become merged among China's struggling millions one lost all volition. As in a pail full of maggots there is a constant seethe— the backwash of those entering and leaving—and just as fresh maggots are constantly coming to the top, so I found myself in a short time at the driver's end of the bus. There was a door there, too, through which I was immediately pressed, and although we had come only a couple of blocks I decided to walk the rest.

Before reaching Urumchi in Chinese Turkestan where I hoped to become once more a traveller, I had first to fly to Lanchow in North China on the Hwang-ho (Yellow River) and then to suffer twelve days in a post-bus. Once a fortnight a plane did the 1200-mile hop from Shanghai to Lanchow in a day. I had difficulty in getting a seat in it, for the Chinese seemed to be over-addicted to air travel. I suppose if one has had much experience of road and rail travel in China, this is what one is apt to become. The advantage of soaring safely over the heads of war-lords and beyond reach of bandits is worth paying for. But it struck me that flying was remarkably cheap. The price of other things seemed to keep well abreast or even ahead of the rapidly falling exchange, but one could fly to Nanking for less than the price of a tin of tobacco.

The war-time transport plane, fitted with iron bucket seats as became the iron-hard seats of the military gentlemen who had formerly used them, left Shanghai at 8 a.m., landed at Hankow, and reached Lanchow that evening. It was the same plane in which an American possessed of much money and considerable hope, had been recently scouring western China in search of a mountain higher than Mt Everest. No doubt on the China-Tibet border there are many unmeasured peaks, indeed parts of the maps of those regions are still largely conjectural, but most of it has been traversed by explorers who, had they noticed such a considerable protuberance as a 30,000 ft. mountain, would certainly have drawn attention to it. On this occasion no mountains higher than 20,000 to 21,000 ft. were seen.

The American pilot was assisted by a Chinese co-pilot whose duties were nominal, part of them being no doubt to save face. He could fly the thing when it was airborne, but, according to the American, he was no great hand at anything else; and since what goes up must at last come down it was a relief to see that this essential ending to a flight was left to the capable hands of the pilot. After flying for some time in cloud, through which one occasionally glimpsed high broken country of hideously eroded, reddish hills, we touched down. I heaved my accustomed sigh of relief:

> So between the starry dome
> And the floor of plain and seas,
> I have never felt at home
> Never really been at ease.

Lanchow-fu, to give it its full name, is the capital of Kansu province. It lies on the right bank of the Hwang-ho at an altitude of 5000 ft. The river is bridged here and it is as a bridge-point on the chief overland approach to China from the West that Lanchow owes its importance from very early times. When I learnt that the nearest railhead was in western Honan twenty-five days' journey away, I felt that the C.N.A.C. (Chinese National Air Corporation) had earned every penny of the fare.

Lanchow was the army headquarters of what was called the 'North West' which included Sinkiang. The commander was General Chang Chi-chung, a man prominent in the peace negotiations after the revolt of the three northern districts of Sinkiang—Ili, Chuguchak, Altai—in 1944, when, having killed or driven out the Chinese troops and civilians, the rebels proclaimed a Republic of East Turkestan. These three districts, half of whose inhabitants are Kazaks, lie to the north of the Tien Shan range and form the wealthiest part of Sinkiang. They produce a surplus of grain, upon which Urumchi is dependent for food, and also oil, gold, wolfram, and coal. Peace terms were negotiated by the General, who became Chairman of a Provincial Coalition Government, but they were never implemented. After more trouble in 1947 a

Turki was appointed Chairman and Chang Chi-chung became commander of the 'North-West'. But Chinese troops were still excluded
from the Ili district, the Chinese had lost all control over it, and in
1948 it was well on the way to becoming another of the Soviet Asiatic
Republics.

However, Chinese writ still ran in Urumchi and the rest of Sinkiang, and the name of the General, to whom I had a letter of introduction, was potent enough there. He was a man who looked a very
fit forty, though I believe he was nearer sixty years old, and he had a
charming wife who had spent several years in England. He gave me
a *laissez-passer* for Sinkiang and a dinner of eight dishes, all as new to
me as the steamed bread and the Russian chocolate with which we
finished. Another powerful ally was the secretary of the China Inland
Mission, a Mr Walker, through whom I obtained a seat in the post-bus
to Urumchi for a modest twenty-eight million dollars. The Lanchow
mission ran a very active hospital situated on the other side of the river.

The town is as nondescript a place as I have seen. All I remember
of it is a steam-roller. I stopped my rickshaw to have a look at this
rara avis whose name, I think, was Hercules. How Hercules had got
himself there from the coast is a question to which I still devote much
thought. The Hwang-ho, known sometimes as China's Sorrow, is not
a traffic artery, a Chinese railway could surely not accommodate him;
had Hercules therefore chugged his way patiently from the coast? If
so, it was surely an example of patient progress and dogged persever-
ance as worthy of an epic poem as the advance of the Chinese army to
the re-conquest of Sinkiang in 1877; when, owing to supply difficulties,
an advance guard had first to plant crops and reap them before the
hungry horde behind could make its next forward spring.

The post-bus service seemed to retain something of the efficiency
and panache of the old courier service, which, when it ran from Sian-fu
in Shensi to Kashgar, was the longest in the world. The drivers of the
big five-ton Dodge truck had the lofty, swaggering airs affected, we are
told, by the drivers of the old flash coaches. They were the aristocrats
of the road, such as it was. Our driver would stroll up at the last minute
smoking a cigarette which he would throw disdainfully to the admiring
onlookers before donning a magnificent pair of white leather gaunt-
lets. He would touch nothing but the driving wheel and that only with

gloves. If anything went wrong, he would dismount to stretch his legs, leaving his two assistants to maltreat the engine and get themselves dirty. Off duty, however, he unbent. We changed driver and crew several times, but I never met one too superior to eat with his mechanics or even with me, and to do them justice they usually paid their bills and mine too. As became mail drivers they did themselves as well as the inns of the road would afford, drank when they could, and played Mah-jong and cards for what looked like great sums of money. Mah-jong, by the way, as played in the inns of the Kansu corridor road by the lorry fraternity, has little resemblance to the laborious, stately wall-building we know. It is played at unnerving pace, the tiles being picked up and banged down with the speed and clatter of a machine gun.

The driver's freedom with his money, while in character with these brothers of the road, could probably be well afforded. Besides his pay there were, I imagine, some trifling perquisites, for in addition to mails the truck carried goods and passengers, who sat comfortably but precariously on top of the load. All, that is, except myself who had the place of honour and discomfort, on the box, as it were. It was cooler on top of the luggage and one could stretch out and sleep. I noticed, however, that no passengers presented themselves at the official starting point where they would presumably have had to buy a ticket. But on the outskirts of the town we usually found waiting for us a small group who had no doubt come to some private arrangement with the driver the previous night. En route we would be frequently 'thumbed' and the driver could pick out instinctively the paying and non-paying 'thumbers'.

When I was not a guest of the driver, which happened only at the midday halt, I found the food question fraught with difficulty and anxiety. Before embarking on this lone journey I had carefully written down phonetically five or six essential words—words, I mean, for food—but there is a wide gulf between the writing and speaking of a foreign tongue and after a few discouraging essays I gave up trying to bridge it. Fortunately, in China there are no ridiculous hygienic regulations for the sale of food, puzzling to the buyer and a hindrance to the seller. It is displayed openly and conveniently in the street, neither behind glass windows, under glass cases, nor, worst of all, in cellophane wrappers. All I had to do therefore was to point to or seize what I wanted and

(6) A pleasant Kanchow suburb; this is the fifth picture taken in Kanchow where I seem to have been a little 'snap-happy', not altogether unsuccessfully

(7)The Dodge mail truck at Suchow; the driver (without his white gloves) leans nonchalantly against the cab; his assistant, in well-cut trousers, is on the left; in between is the Postmaster; the bonnet of the truck has been removed to allow more air and more dust to reach the engine flourish some notes; and the stall-keeper, mistaking me for a wealthy deaf-mute, complied with alacrity. Still, I like to get value for money, even Chinese paper money, and at first it was difficult to know whether to tender 10,000 dollars or half a million for a piece of bread. If the man was honest, and most of them were, one found oneself either with a derisory portion or with more than one could carry away.

This method, of course, restricted one to *al fresco* feeding; good enough in its way, but there were times when I wanted to get my legs under a table and to probe more deeply into the mysteries of Chinese food. As befits a civilized race the Chinese regard food with commendable gravity and have some unusual ideas about what may be eaten and how it should be cooked. It was quite maddening, therefore, for me to see and smell these bizarre and possibly pleasing dishes in preparation and not to be able to ask for them. As the only barbarian then on view I was everywhere a conspicuous figure and was therefore followed generally by a small crowd. If I went into an eating-house, the crowd came too to watch the fun. In a place where the cooking and eating go on in the same room it should be easy to get what one wants, but watched by a hundred eyes I found the process too embarrassing. If, on the other hand, I managed to sneak in unobserved and sat down expectantly at the first table, I found myself either ignored or subjected to a volley of uncouth sound. No one had the nous to plank down in front of me something edible. Perhaps they thought, not unreasonably, that I had merely come to study the habits of the flies.

When hunger did eventually drive me to confront these obstacles to the eating of a square meal I found 'a trifling sum of misery new added to the foot of my account'. For when the guest at a Chinese eating-house finally lays down his tooth-pick with a sigh, pays his bill, and quits the table, the waiter in a strident bawl announces to the remaining clients the amount of the bill and the size of the proffered tip. The shades of meaning which can be expressed by the voice, even when uttering some bald figures, are no less numerous than the inferences suggested by a restaurant bill. Until custom has made him brazen, the fear that he has been publicly tried and found guilty of either extravagance or meanness, gluttony or crapulence, will in turn cross the mind of the replete but unhappy guest as he bolts for the door. I suppose this is done so that the owner of the 'joint', ensconced behind a pile of rice, can jot down the amount taken by his various waiters. Obviously it saves labour and book-keeping, and since publicity or the fear of publicity is a powerful monitor, the system is one worth the attention of a Minister of Food in any Welfare State.

The road crossed the river, quitted it, and climbed to a 10,000 ft. pass where snow still lingered on the hills above. At this season the river was rising, fast-flowing, and of a dirty yellow colour (hence the name Yellow River) owing to the quantity of yellow loess soil carried down in suspension. The Yellow Sea into which the great river flows is presumably so called on account of its discoloration by river water. The hills of north-west China consist for the most part of thick deposits of loess which, according to Prof. Albrecht Penck (*Geog. Jour.* vol. 76), were derived from mud brought by the Hwang-ho from Central Asia during the Ice Age. The loess is being constantly eroded by rivers to form numerous gorges and the yellow soil is then carried to the plains whence it is again swept up by the wind and redeposited elsewhere. The loess haze to which this process gives rise is most marked in west Sinkiang where more often than not visibility is limited to a few miles only. This haziness occurs on even perfectly still days so that one might almost believe the loess dust to be so fine and impalpable as to be equally at home in the air or on the ground.

Von Richthofen was the first to recognise loess as an aeolian deposit. He made a series of remarkable journeys in China in the 1870s, and we were presently to catch sight of that part of the Nan Shan range between Kanchow and Suchow which has been named after him. We reached Kanchow the second night about 320 miles out. At many points we had passed close to the still impressive remains of the Great Wall on the north side of the road, and Kanchow was a typical Chinese walled town. The Chinese have a sublime faith in walls, even to this day. Apart from the Great Wall, their earliest architectural monument still above ground, cities and towns must be surrounded by walls. In China, no wall no town is axiomatic. At all the towns that I passed sentries paced these walls, the guards had their quarters in them, and at night the great wooden gates in the massive arched gateways were solemnly shut. These town walls are solid; a core of earth and stone covered with unburnt brick, 20–30 ft. high, and wide enough on top for a cart to be driven.

(8) The truck in mid-Gobi; 'My beautiful, my beautiful... Fret not to roam the desert now with all thy winged speed;' the telephone pole (back right) is as fatal to Romance as the truck, but without them the picture would be singularly vacant

(9) The tombs of the Hami princes with high domes of green glazed tiles and blue and white tiled walls; the surrounding walls are the usual clay pisé work which in dry climates lasts for a long time: e.g., the Great Wall of China

Walls are considered efficacious not only against the outer barbarians—Mongolian hordes and such like—but also against evilly disposed devils. A few feet inside the entrance to a Chinese compound there is often built a piece of wall* rather longer than the width of the entrance, so that anyone entering the compound has to make two right-angled turns. Such a device is quite devil-proof, for devils move only in straight lines. It is said, and I like to believe it, that the strongest objection to the building of the first railways in China was on the grounds that such remarkably long, straight lines would facilitate the movement of devils. I noticed these walls mostly in the compounds of government buildings which are rightly held to be more devil-ridden than any others.

Kanchow (2–6) was a place of life and colour where the modern bazaar street was happily obscured by the neighbouring old-style houses, willow trees, and temples, of which the principal is the Hall of the Sleeping Buddha which for size almost rivalled the famous one at Bangkok. The Buddha is 120 ft. long and 40 ft. high, constructed of hollow clay, painted and lacquered. Whatever the old houses may have been like inside they looked delightful from without, with their curly projecting roofs of warm glazed tiles and elaborately carved eaves and supporting brackets. I have heard a theory that the curling concave roofs of Chinese buildings derive from the shape of Mongol tents (5). But the normal Mongol tent is the yort with a sensibly convex roof, the sagging ridge-pole type of tent being used only when on the move. Moreover, Chinese culture is quite alien to Mongolian; nor is it easy to see why the Chinese, who were building pagodas hundreds of years before the rise of the Mongolian Empire, should have been indebted to those widespreading, hard-riding ruffians for any architectural ideas except perhaps that of a stout wall for keeping them out. Such obscure, insoluble questions, however, are best left to sinologists for whom they provide a smouldering slag-heap of conjecture and controversy, which is ever ready to blaze anew at the wind of some fresh archaeological find.

---

* These walls are known as 'pi-hsia-ch'iang' or 'avoidance of uncanny influence wall' (Lattimore).

CHAPTER II

TO URUMCHI

To SUCHOW IN THREE DAYS was good going. We had averaged 150 miles a day until a halt here of four days spoilt our average and checked my rising admiration for the Chinese Postal Service. However, a stay of four days at 'The Spring of Wine', as Suchow is known, should have sounded gratefully in the ears of anyone but an anchorite; but the poetical extravagance of Chinese place-names was for me already suspect and the drab appearance of the town did nothing to allay that suspicion.

Having been rebuilt on a new site after the destruction of the old town during the Tungan (Chinese Moslem) rebellion of 1860, it lacked the old houses, temples, and trees of a place like Kanchow which had successfully resisted the rebels. The rebuilding had evidently been in the hands of a barbarian town planner, for it was laid out in the convenient but dull criss-cross style. 'The Spring of Wine', which is outside the present walls, proved to be as pleasant as its name. I found it a large walled garden, so informal as to be almost a wilderness, with reed-filled ponds and melancholy willows, moss-grown temples, grottos, and paths, all surrounding a stone basin in which a limpid spring was bubbling. In a shady arbour by the spring were stone seats where one could sit and drink tea.

Marco Polo once passed through Suchow; as had Benedict Goez, the lay Jesuit traveller, 'who had sought Cathay and found heaven'. Leaving the court of Akbar in 1603 Benedict Goez went by the upper Oxus and over the Pamirs to Yarkand and Khotan, and finally to Suchow where in 1607, after being detained for sixteen months, he died of disease and privation just as aid reached him. Marco Polo dismisses Suchow in half a page and wastes little more on Kanchow where he spent a whole year. But a first journey, like a first ascent, needs no embellishment; the thing either speaks for itself or there is so much to be told that there is neither room nor need for digression. Subsequent travellers, on the contrary, to make amends for any lack of novelty must needs digress often at the risk of losing their reader's attention; just as the climber on a hackneyed crag seeks for novelty at more serious hazard.

When the driver dropped me and my kit in the Post Office compound and advised me to 'scram', I was at a loss. The best of prospects is improved by an inn, but here was neither prospect nor inn. I looked at one and recoiled in dismay at the thought of spending four nights there—an example of 'the initiate fear which wants hard use' and which was later to be got at the inns of Hami and other places. Very reluctantly I billeted myself upon two American ladies of the C.I.M. who kindly took me in, although their house, which was being rebuilt, was all at sixes and sevens.

According to Stevenson, a taste for general information, not promptly checked, had sapped Uncle Joseph's manhood. Air and bus travel were sapping mine; hoping to restore it I tramped the uninteresting, flat countryside where I could walk abroad without becoming a public portent. Shod in climbing boots I walked far and fast, taking my lunch of steamed bread with meagre date-filling off the last barrow-boy's pitch without the city wall. Poor anaemic stuff it was, too, not to be compared with the rough Turki bread obtainable further west. That the confines of China were not far off was evident, for Tibetans were occasionally to be seen in the streets, and the black tents of nomads with their yaks and camels outside the walls.

Although Urumchi was still 700 miles away I managed to speak by telephone with Mr Paxton the American Consul with whom Shipton would be staying. A long-distance telephone call always impresses me as something of an achievement both by myself and by Alexander Graham Bell, and this last feat pleased and astonished me. There is no reason, of course, why the noise a Chinese makes should not be as acceptable to a telephone instrument as any of the more recognised forms of speech; but I am still puzzled as to how telegrams are handled in a language that has no alphabet.

A compulsory visit to the police station in accordance with the Suchow immigration bylaws led to my meeting a young student who had some English. He asked me to dine and I gladly accepted, for restaurants had no terror for me when accompanied by an habitué. We

went to the upstairs room of a place chosen with some care. It had
not struck me before, but there were degrees of dirtiness in the restaurant world of Kansu and my companion was more fastidious than
I. It would not have been in Dr Johnson's opinion a dinner to *ask* a
man to. It consisted of spaghetti laced with bean sauce or red pepper
according to choice, which is the common eating-house dish called
'kua mien'. The equipment is equally simple, a bowl, a saucer for the
sauce, chopsticks; and to wipe the latter in case they had not been
washed, the proprietor provided, regardless of expense, two bits of
paper. Fans could be borrowed gratis and one could spit on the floor
if one wished—Liberty Hall, in fact. To finish we had what sounded to
me like 'champagne' tea which implied the most expensive kind. It was
heavily flavoured and since the ordinary tea was not flavoured at all, in
future I always asked for 'champagne'.

The bus did not leave until the fifth day, but partially made up
for lost time with a run of 170 miles to Anhsi. At a place called Chia-
yu-Kuan (Barrier of the Pleasant Valley) just west of Suchow the road
passes through the remains of the western extremity of the Great Wall.
This was the western limit of the old Middle Kingdom, China 'Within
the Wall'. The wall here is of puddled clay about twelve feet thick and
twenty high. The late Sir Aurel Stein has shown that west of Suchow
there were in fact two walls. One dating from the second century B.C.
continued westwards to Tunhuang beyond Anhsi; its purpose being
to protect the narrow line of oases strung along the foot of the Nan
Shan (the South Mountains) which were indispensable as a means of
commercial and political advance into Central Asia. The second wall,
of far more recent construction, was built for the opposite purpose,
to close the Central Asian route at a time when China was on the
defensive.

In the early afternoon we reached Yu-men-hsien, the 'Town of
the Jade Gate'. We remained here until 6 p.m. to avoid the heat of the
desert lying between us and Anhsi. This section of desert, by the way,
provided the best running of the day. In two fat, fascinating volumes,
Ruins of Desert Cathay, Sir Aurel Stein describes how he found the ruins
of the west wall of Tunhuang and how having first dug up a reference
to 'Jade Gate', at length located the actual fort in the neighbourhood
of Tunhuang.

(10) This butcher's stall in Hami has on its long array of meat-hooks
some fleshless ribs and three scraggy legs of goat—a butcher's shop
in England in A.D. 1950 cannot display much more

(11) The massive facade of the Central Bank of China, Urumchi, is of the solid, expensive, confidence-inspiring type of architecture desirable for banks everywhere and nowhere more so than in Urumchi

Among our first finds [he writes] was a label evidently once tied to a bag, referring to a hundred bronze arrowheads and naming a certain company of 'Yu-men'. So at last I had found the name of that famous Jade Gate which I had thought from the first was to be located somewhere along this westernmost part of the 'limes'. Again and again in the course of subsequent excavations I felt grateful for the *amor scribendi* which seems to have prompted these ancient 'military Babus'—like those whom one now meets in queer corners of the fortified posts scattered along the Indian North-West Frontier—to beguile their ennui and demonstrate their own importance by a constant flow of reports, store statements, and other documents so familiar to soldiering men in most regions.

And later he goes on:

The thinnest layer of gravel sufficed to preserve in absolute freshness even such perishable objects as shreds of clothing, wooden tablets, arrow-shafts, straw, and chips. Whatever objects had once passed under this protection were practically safe in a soil which had seen but extremely scanty rainfall for the last two thousand years, was far removed from any chance of irrigation or other interference by human agency, and had suffered on its flat surface but rarely even from wind erosion. Often a mere scraping with my boot-heel sufficed to disclose where the detachments holding the posts had been accustomed to throw their refuse. With all the reports, statements, and enquiries which a fully developed and, no doubt, scribe-ridden military organization had kept moving along this chain of border watch-stations for more than two thousand years, was it wonderful that I soon grew accustomed to picking up records of the time of Christ or before, almost on the surface?

We did not reach Anhsi, the 'West-protecting', until late at night and though we left again at 5 a.m. it was no hardship for me who had to pass the short night on the Post Office counter. Nor would the tourist have missed anything, for crumbling city walls and one wide dilapidated street made up the sum total of Anhsi. And here I must enter a protest at the mutability of Chinese place-names, attributable sometimes to change of government and sometimes to change of mind on the part of scholars. How is one to travel to the right place or even write about it when Anhsi may be Ngan-hsi or Anhsichow; Kanchow equally Chang-yeh; and Suchow Chin-chu'an? Most flagrant of all is Peiping for what most of us go on calling Peking. This was one of the far-reaching reforms carried out in 1928 when the Nationalist armies took the place and transferred the capital to Nanking. Nor was this the only change made. Practically every street in Shanghai, and there are a good many, was renamed, but the old names had been in use so long that to this day a street map is provided with a key showing the original names. This itch to efface old memories is a habit that has derived, with many other bad habits, from the French Revolution. It is high time some public-spirited man called a meeting of prospective revolutionaries and persuaded them to pass a Self-Denying Ordinance that whatever other violent changes they might have in view, all place-names, especially those of mountains, should be sacrosanct.

Anhsi was formerly important as the junction of two great routes to the West, south and north respectively of the Tarim basin. And it was by the control of the Tarim basin through the occupation of Sin-kiang that China kept open this essential road. The old road, which we had followed as far as Anhsi, passed along the southern edge of the Lop Nor and Takla Makhan desert (both part of the Tarim basin) to Khotan, Yarkand, Kashgar, and thence either north of the Pamirs or south through Wakhan to Bokhara and Samarkand. In Marco Polo's day this route had almost been abandoned in favour of one which struck north-west from Anhsi across a part of the Gobi desert to Hami and thence along the north side of the Tarim basin to Kashgar. This last is the present motor road, but recently there was some talk of making the old southern route practicable for lorries.

The missionary authors of *Through Jade Gate and Central Asia* who have vividly described the Gobi desert do well to lament the gradual ousting of the camel caravan by motor transport—a process which, beginning in the thirties, has accelerated rapidly during the war. Poets see what others miss. It is all very well for Kipling to write of Romance bringing up the nine-fifteen, but to my prosaic mind a truck is a vehicle fatal to Romance (8). The more wild and lonely the environment, the more incongruous and romance-shattering is the presence of a truck;

(12) The main street, Urumchi; the blue-hooded shandrydan is drawn
by a pony harnessed in Russian fashion

(13) Urumchi bazaar; the old bearded Turkoman on the left is still wearing his cotton-quilted 'chapan', while the Turki on the right wears a summer gown of white cotton; between them is a Chinese soldier and the mounted man is a Chinese officer

although the desert may hold something of the grandeur and terror
of the sea, in the desert these qualities are more easily dissipated by
mechanical transport. The desert may have moods, but it never can
assume the aggressive violence of the sea, which can so easily reduce
machinery to scrap-iron and impotence. True, trucks often break down
in the desert—'It is but machinery, Sahib,' as an apologetic Indian
driver reminded me—but these misfortunes cannot be ascribed to its
wrath. Nor if they break down are they in any danger of foundering or
driving ashore. On the whole, I think that Romance in travel is inseparable from an element of risk:

> My mistress still the open road
> And the bright eyes of danger.

Perhaps too early and heavy a breakfast of bread gave rise to this melancholy train of thought as we chugged slowly away from Anhsi across
the desert, where the scene was indeed favourable for Romance if only
the smell of petrol could have been excluded. The mind might spread
its melancholy freely as the desert which on our right hand stretched
to the bitter Mongolian steppes, and on our left to the thirsty sand
of the Lop Nor; for the sun had not yet risen to redeem a little the
harsh unfriendliness of this gravel wilderness in which the ragged outline of jet-black hills appeared like islands rising from a sombre sea.
That deserts are rarely sandy was a fact which impressed itself upon
me during the late war when we careered across the Syrian and Sinai
deserts in a matter of days, and then for six months rolled backwards
and forwards, rather less lightheartedly, across the desert of Libya,
where gravel is the rule and pockets of sand the exception. Nor need
they be flat; the scorched and scarred mountains on either side of the
Red Sea at once come to mind, and here in the Gobi we often had to
wind through defiles between low rocky hills.

We left Kansu and entered Sinkiang at a place in mid-desert,
Hsinghsingsia, where we stopped the night. It was full of police and
soldiers in marching order, more powerful dissipators of Romance
even than trucks. I slept at the Post Office where I had lunched in
a pretty lordly way with the driver and other high officials. It was
brought to us from some no doubt squalid inn and I noticed that a
fantastic amount of paper was handed over in exchange. In the middle

of the Gobi one must expect to pay for one's pleasure. But one might have hoped that in a country of harsh facts, where man existed only on sufferance, so remote from treasuries and banks, that the man-made mystery of exchange rates would have been unknown. Nevertheless, for reasons best known perhaps to some bland financial wizard fanning himself at Hong Kong, the Sinkiang dollar or 'kuchen' was worth five Chinese dollars. Thus, since the money was the same, until one got used to multiplying or dividing by five one was constantly being cheated or detected in a cheat.

We left early, fresh and fasting. The road climbed to a pass and then began dropping steadily to a flat plain of gravel and hard clay where the heat began to increase noticeably. Having broken our fast in the company of some soldiers at a Chinese post we drove rapidly westwards at the foot of the distant snow-covered Karlik Tagh until in the late afternoon we reached the prosperous oasis of Hami. As there was some doubt about when we should go on, I had to find quarters. At the third inn I tried, either from curiosity or pity, they took me in.

Much has been written about the inns of China and Sinkiang, little of it to their credit. It should be remembered, however, that those who write about these inns were never expected to stay in them. They are meant for travellers whose wants are conspicuously few, whose luggage consists of a little tobacco or opium, and who do not regard the presence of a few bugs (a weak point in these inns) as an indictable offence. They are part and parcel of the country.

The 'Inn of the Overlapping Teeth' at which I stopped was happily named because it was only a sleeping inn. That is to say you were given a mud room or cell and nothing else. In my cell I seem to remember a table, but as there was never anything put upon it, not even an aspidistra, it was purely symbolic. The bed was the usual raised earth dais with a fire-place underneath for heating in winter; very naturally the bed had become the ancestral home of not a few bugs. A little sweeping and watering to lay the dust and one's bed is made; and should one be addicted to washing then there is a well in one corner of the serai. 'Simplify, simplify', as Thoreau constantly urged.

The traveller or the reader of travel books who reaches Hami will find the matter of place-names becoming even more troublesome. Now in addition to the Chinese name with all its variants, there is a Turki name also with scholarly variations. Hami is the Chinese name, Kumul or Qomul the Turki. Marco Polo in his swift way discussed Camul, as he calls it, in three paragraphs devoted largely to the people and their manners, which a traveller might condone but which a moralist must certainly condemn:

> They are a people who take things very easily, for they mind nothing but playing and singing, and dancing and enjoying themselves... And it is the truth that if a foreigner comes to the house of one of these people to lodge the host is delighted, and desires his wife to put herself entirely at the guest's disposal, while he himself gets out of the way. The guest may stay and enjoy the wife's society as long as he likes while the husband has no shame in the matter, but indeed considers it an honour. And all the men of his province are made wittols of by their wives in this manner. The wives themselves are fair and wanton.

Hami has always been important to the Chinese as a commercial centre and as a base for the frequent reconquests of Sinkiang which they have been obliged to undertake. Early in the seventeenth century Hami came under the Moslem Khan or Prince of Kashgar, and until recently it was nominally a political entity ruled by a Khan of its own just as Khiva and Bokhara once were. The Chinese recovered it in 1720, lost it during the Moslem rebellion of 1865, and recovered it again in 1873. There are now three towns—the Chinese walled town containing barracks and government offices, a modern hybrid bazaar, and the old walled city of Kumul of narrow alley-ways containing the palace of the Khan.

Having put through another call to Urumchi to report progress, and having had a hair-cut (70,000 kuchen), I took once more to walking—the alternative to lying in my cell brushing away flies and curious visitors. But I found the country ill-suited to walking for pleasure. No matter which direction one took, sooner rather than later one struck a dry, flat, gravelly plain without landmarks or objectives of any kind. Mounted upon a horse is the way to enjoy this sort of country, and then only if the horse is a free-moving, generous beast and not the usual dull hireling fobbed off upon strangers. Until it gets bored a horse is inspired rather than depressed by an unbroken expanse of flat gravel. Wild ancestral memories of boundless freedom take possession of it, giving great satisfaction to the rider in whom speed of movement fosters the false impression that presently he will see something new.

As there was still no activity at the Post Office, another day had to be spent in aimless wandering. Not quite aimless, however, for on my way out of the town I visited the tombs of the Hami princes (9), which with their high domes of green glazed tiles and blue and white tiled walls were well worth seeing. As usual I took a lunch of bread with me. Without a chaperon I preferred to avoid the rubs and forgo the delights of eating in the town (10), for having poked about the bazaar pretty thoroughly I had become almost a national figure and now avoided it whenever possible. In Hami, as everywhere else, there is nothing funnier than a foreigner. I noticed that ice was on sale which, from its worn, dirty appearance, might well have been a relic of the Ice Age, but which is, I suppose, gathered in winter and stored in icehouses.

A great deal of rice is grown, also grapes, and the melons for which Hami is famous. They used to be sent to the Imperial Court at Peking. Such a journey must have taken the ordinary caravan about three months, so perhaps the melon began its honourable journey as a seedling in a pot of Hami soil and finished it fully ripe for the Imperial stomach. Or ripe melons might have gone by relays of couriers, for in his book *High Tartary* Lattimore speaks of Bara-kul ponies (Bara-kul is a lake north-west of Hami) which can do 100 miles a day; or, perhaps, dried melons were sent, for in the intense summer heat of this region melons can be dried before they rot. In my opinion these melons were not worth so much trouble. Although luscious enough, they were not the equals of the best of Kashgar—the 'beshak shirin', for example, which is a yellowy green canteloupe of exquisite flavour.

When I went round to the Post Office that evening and interrupted a brisk Mah-jong session I learnt that we would go that night. In summer the lorry drivers do as much night driving as they can owing to the heat which becomes ever fiercer until the Turfan Depression is reached and passed. We left at 11 p.m. and stopped forty miles on to sleep on the road. By 6 a.m. we were off again and twelve hours later had reached Chiktam nearly 200 miles from Hami. The road clung to the foothills of the Karlik Tagh which are an easterly extension of the

(14) Taoist shrine near the north end of the Tien Shih lake; the path
which passes the shrine lies over the top of an immense and very old
moraine which closes the north end of the lake

(15) The Heavenly Pool—Tien Shih lake, 'a great sheet of deepest sapphire water'; according to Merzbacher it is about 700 metres deep and the water temperature in August 50° F; had we been aware of these two frightening figures we should neither have boated nor bathed

Bogdo Ola, separated from it by a narrow gap through which there is a pass to the north. Having climbed nearly to the gap at a height of about 4000 ft. the road turned south-west away from the mountains and ran down to the plains. All this is even more desert-like country than the Gobi, and there are even fewer posts and wells.

We carried on till 11 p.m., slept a few hours, and finished the remaining forty miles to Turfan before 6 a.m. Of Turfan, which looked interesting, I was not allowed to see much, for after some delicious hot bread and tea with the postmaster we were off again at 8 a.m. One Turfan peculiarity which I had already noticed on the way was the long lines of spoil from the wells of the 'karez'.

This underground system of irrigation practised by the Turkis of the Turfan Depression is unknown to the Chinese who in any case do not occupy themselves with agriculture in Sinkiang. They come to this Chinese colony not as settlers, but as soldiers, officials, or traders. The 'karez' was introduced from Persia in the eighteenth century. It consists of a series of wells tapping an underground flow of water. The furthest well is sunk until water is reached and then a series of wells of diminishing depth (owing to the slope of the ground) are dug at intervals of about ten yards. An underground tunnel is then driven to connect the whole series so that the water finally emerges at ground level beyond the last well. The wells facilitate the digging of the tunnel and the cleaning of it. All the people of Turfan are not dependent on 'karez' water, for water is also obtained from streams that drain from the southern glaciers of Bogdo Ola—streams which, having disappeared under the gravel plain at the foot of the mountain, reappear from the red sandstone hills bordering the depression on the north.

Turfan town is about 250 ft. above sea level, while the lowest point in the Depression, some thirty miles south, is 426 ft. below sea level. Outside the basin the ground rises rapidly to 2500 ft. The soil is loess which, except in the lowest parts where it is saline, is extremely fertile wherever water can be brought. Rice, cotton, wheat, grapes, melons, and vegetables of all kinds grow to perfection. The piles of prime fruit and vegetables displayed in the mat-shaded bazaar gladdened the heart; but even for the sake of eating its produce I should not wish to live in Turfan, except in winter. Besides shading their streets with mats, trellises, and vines, the people employ whole fleets of donkeys for the carriage of water which is flung lavishly over floors, walls, and streets to mitigate the parching heat. By nine of a morning the busy streets fall silent and the shady marketplace is abandoned to flies and sleeping donkeys.

The long gruelling climb out of the Depression up the steep gravel glacis in the heat of the day sorely tried our labouring engine which threatened constantly to boil over. Still climbing, we entered a gorge with a dry river bed; then a few willow thickets appeared, bits of grass; and soon without quite realising how the trick had been performed we found we were winding along the verdant banks of a laughing river. The gorge opened, and as though crossing a pass we debouched upon a green plain. On our right the grass soon yielded to another great gravel glacis scored with dry water-courses, and above the glacis rose the steep ramparts of Bogdo Ola, castellated with ice and snow. At a good inn at Davanchin (Dawan Ch'eng, the City of the Pass) some thirty miles from Urumchi, I ate for the last time with the crew of the lorry. From the upstairs room I watched the clouds form and dissolve about the great mountain which, I thought, looked decidedly hostile.

We drove on, the now cloud-hidden mountain far on our right and on our left a broad, blue, reed-fringed lake without visible inlet or outlet; I was elated both with the glimpse of the noble mountain I had come so far to see and by the long-looked-for meeting in this distant country with an old tried friend. The journey had been long and more tiring than it should have been: for I had been from the start a passenger and not a traveller, with neither animals to care for nor porters to cajole.

At last, ten miles from Urumchi, I saw a familiar truck and by it a familiar figure. Two familiar figures, in fact, for Mr Shipton had with him his Sherpa servant Lakhpa who had been with us in our disastrous attempt upon Muztagh Ata the previous year. Ready hands took charge of my scanty luggage, and as the Dodge trundled onwards towards the now setting sun the gratitude I felt was only tempered by the regret that the old ways of travel had been almost extinguished by the truck and its kind.

(16) 'Across the lake and above the pines shone the splendour of the
new mountain world that we had come to visit'

(17) Greeson and his White Russian ply the one and a half oars; his battery and boots are stacked in the bows where the water level is lowest; as any mariner will see, she is a chine-built craft; i.e., angular, without flowing lines

CHAPTER III

BOGDO OLA

———————◆———————

U RUMCHI IS A FINE OUTLANDISH NAME for a town, a name whose
richness and raffish promise makes the Chinese name of Tiwha
sound thin and prim. That celebrated list of places at which Uncle
Joseph settled his imaginary recipient of £80 a year when he lectured
to the Working Men's Institute, Isle of Dogs, on how to live on that
amount, would, I think, have rolled more richly from the tongue had
Urumchi replaced, say, Brighton: 'London, Paris, Bagdad, Spitzber-
gen, Bussorah, Heligoland, the Scilly Isles, Urumchi, Cincinnati, and
Nijni Novgorod.' My feeling that it belied its promise of rollicking iniq-
uity might have been unjust, but I only spent a few days there—many
more are needed before one should pass judgment on such a place. And
who can say what went on behind the high walls of the Russian Consulate, for example; in the Chinese yamen of the new town; or, above
all, behind the massive facade of the Central Bank of China (11), which
was of the expensive, solid, confidence-inspiring type of architecture,
an incongruous building to see rising amid a huddle of unburnt brick
and corrugated iron.

The American Consulate, where Shipton and I were grateful
guests, had neither the aloof mysterious air of Russia nor the opulent
magnificence of the Bank. The Americans had established their Consulate only during the last war (1943), whereas the Russians were almost
coeval with the resumption of power by the Chinese in Sinkiang in
the latter part of the last century. Hence they had not had the time to
buy or build something more worthy of the present inheritors of the
White Man's Burden—at any rate of his financial burden. The Consulate buildings were in a side-street on the outskirts, and hard by was
the four-roomed establishment destined for the British Consul and his
family then on their way from Shanghai. This is a lodging well suited
to a representative of the New Poor when they at last give up their
ideas on keeping up appearances.

51

But whatever the American Consulate may have looked from outside, there was a great amount of activity and hospitality inside. Seldom less than a dozen people took breakfast there. In addition to the staff and a fellow-consul like Shipton, who without straining the imagination could be said to be there on business, there were myself, who by no stretch of imagination had any business at all, two or three American officials and visitors, and above all American journalists. The latter were always coming and going, relentlessly interviewing, and persistently acquiring information with which to rear edifices of theory upon the shifting sands of Central Asian politics. The great question then (by now resolved) was whether the revolted province of Ili would return to the Chinese fold or whether it would remain under the increasing Russian influence.

We gave ourselves three days to put our affairs in order—to pay our respects to Chinese officials, to pack, and to collect food for our three weeks' excursion to Bogdo Ola. Mrs Paxton, the wife of the American Consul, gave us the run of her overflowing store, and although we may have tried to sustain an undeserved reputation for austerity there is little doubt that we failed. I, at any rate, seldom make the vulgar mistake of not taking enough, if it is enough only of unvarnished bellytimber such as flour or rice; which is, no doubt, what the Chinese sage had in mind when he affirmed that a well-filled stomach is indeed the great thing—all else is luxury. Nearly all climbers would agree with the first part of this proposition, but might wish to make reservations about the second. I say nearly all because I have in mind one of the early climbers of Mont Blanc who advised a friend with similar ambitions that 'provisions are of no use, all that is wanted is an umbrella and a scent bottle'.

The food of an expedition is governed largely by questions of transport and since in most serious expeditions transport is likely to be difficult it should be taken as a general rule that the food should be austerely simple—bare necessities, in fact, like flour and sugar which require no other packing than a sack. Hence it is a seductive, convincing, and possibly sound argument—one that I find myself using too often—that the only good reason for cutting out all the luxuries and most of the comforts of life is the difficulty of transport. If, the argument goes, the expedition is not likely to encounter these

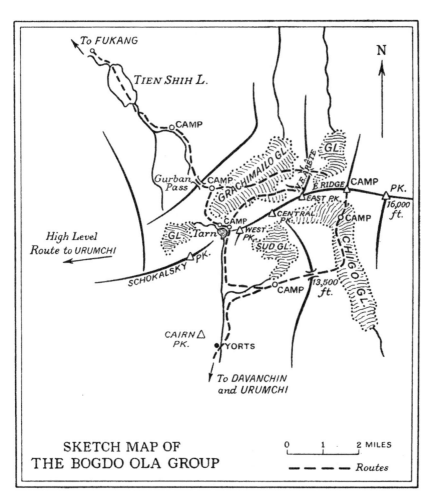

To FUKANG

TIEN SHIH L.

N

CAMP

Gurban
Pass

CAMP

GRACHIMAILO GL.

N.E. ARÊTE

GL.

E. RIDGE

CAMP

EAST PK.

PK.

16,000
ft.

High Level
Route to URUMCHI

GL. Tarn

CAMP

WEST
PK.

CENTRAL
PK.

CAMP

CHIGO GL.

SUD GL.

SCHOKALSKY

PK.

CAMP

13,500
ft.

CAIRN
PK.

YORTS

To DAVANCHIN
and URUMCHI

SKETCH MAP OF
THE BOGDO OLA GROUP

0   1   2 MILES

— — — Routes

Map 2: The Bogda Ola Group

difficulties—the English of which is that you will not have to carry any load yourself—then there is no very urgent call to practise austerity. Let yaks grunt, porters sweat, and donkeys quiver at the knees, but let there be enough luxuries in the way of butter, jam, cheese, marmalade etc. to help down the humdrum necessities of flour and rice. After all—applying theory to practice—Bogdo Ola was a mere thirty miles by lorry road, whence ponies would carry our belongings easily to the foot of the mountain, so why quibble over a few glass jars of peanut butter (the glass weighing considerably more than the contents) or whether to take five or six 2 lb. tins of marmalade? If it is true, as Dr Johnson observed, that abstinence is not a virtue in itself but only the groundwork of a virtue, it is a thing the high-souled man can afford to ignore.

Urumchi lies athwart all roads to the east or to the west, on which account alone, I imagine, is it the capital, for any other merits are not easily discernible. Roads lead to China either north or south of the Bogdo Ola group; a road leads to Outer Mongolia, another to Russia by Ili or by Chuguchak, and there is the road to Kashgar south of the Tien Shan. As befits a capital it is thus a commercial centre and a focal point for travellers and their tales; some of which are authentic, but the majority are merely rumours of a most lurid kind. Although the important Ili road had long been closed on account of the revolt, the Turki bazaar was still a lively place, much livelier than the Chinese shopping centre in the new town—the Chinese city proper (12)—where a lot of American and European fountain pens, watches, torches, and so on were for sale at fancy prices.

Besides poking about in the bazaar (13), looking at jade cups and ornamented whips and speculating on the queer vegetables and spices on offer—for wheresoever any particular herb grows there lives the ass who is to eat it—we spent much time bathing in a newly constructed reservoir five miles out, or vainly trying to get a shot at the duck and geese which occasionally visited it. So pleasant was this lake that I even used to trot out there before breakfast, partly to fettle up and partly to exorcise the combined effects of American and Chinese hospitality. Apart from the constant knife-and-fork play at the Consulate and an occasional chop-stick match against the Chinese, the American Military Attache and his wife, who were also visitors, liked to have informal

(18) The Kazak yort pitched on a grassy shoulder (*c*. 8000 ft.) where we camped; even the back view of Lakhpa suggests that he is inclining to stoutness; Hill Billy, facing him, is marked by his white Hunza cap; the elaborate head-dresses of the women are distinctive, and the figure on the left which at first glance I took for myself, I now recognise, with the help of a magnifying glass, as the Kazak chief; the dark patches on the opposing slope are juniper bushes

(19) Kazaks in Urumchi bazaar; contrary to rule this particular pair
of centaurs have dismounted; their long fur-trimmed helmets seem
to be without their crowning glory, the tuft of feathers

snack parties at odd hours—a purée of red chilli spread on biscuits, grapes, raw paprika, Turki bread, and peaches, all of which needed to be assuaged with the local rice brandy or Russian vodka. It might be thought that using a weapon as ineffective looking as a chop-stick, would prevent anything more than polite pecking, but with a little practice it is surprising how much one can rake, claw, or shovel in. The postmaster, who was from Canton, gave us a dinner of Cantonese food which in China is regarded as *hors concours*. Fried oysters on lettuce perhaps qualified as a 'dish to be eaten on one's knees'; but the custom of drinking tea before dinner and brandy throughout is, like marriage, rather to be permitted than approved.

But enough, something too much, of these low pleasures; especially when one may see, as we did, on leaving the house of a morning, a far-off tower of ice and snow, severe in outline, but warm and friendly in the rising sun. Having loaded the truck overnight we left early on 10 July for Fukang some forty miles away.

The climbing party consisted of four: Shipton and myself, the perhaps slightly blunted spearhead of the attack; Lakhpa, a Sherpa, who was Shipton's major domo, factotum, and knowledgeable adviser in mundane affairs; and a Hunza man whose name other than that of 'Hill Billy' by which we knew him has escaped me.

Lakhpa had been with Shipton or me on several Himalayan journeys, notably on Everest in 1938 when he had carried to Camp VI, and afterwards on the return home he had accompanied me over the Zemu Gap. He had gone to Kashgar in 1940 when Shipton did his first spell there as Consul. He had taken very readily to life in Kashgar, and through his zeal for his master's affairs and his own he had now acquired an influential position among the menial staff of the Consulate, a Turki wife, and a great belly. The Chinese saying that no honest official has fat subordinates carries, in this case, the doctrine of collective responsibility too far. Anyway, what mattered was not Lakhpa's honesty but his obesity which we feared might now prevent his carrying our loads. The Hunza man was one of the Kashgar mail couriers on the Kashgar-Tashkurgan run. He looked cheerful, tough, keen, and had come perhaps under the mistaken impression that he was on holiday. He was not much given to idle chat, but that may have been because we had no common language.

Fukang is on the north road to Hami and the east which lies along the edge of the Zungarian plain and the foothills of Bogdo Ola. Not far from Urumchi there are some coal measures where open-cast mining is carried on in a desultory way. At Fukang we expected to find ponies ready to take us the same day as far as the lake of Tien Shih (Heavenly Pool), but the enthusiastic promises made to us at Urumchi had not yet been translated into action at Fukang. We must take the truck on as far as we could and hope that ponies would be sent up that evening. By noon we had reached the end of the rough road well among the foothills, and from there we manhandled the loads to a pleasant camp by water and willows and settled down to await our transport.

At dark they arrived, and with them, in a jeep, Greeson of the American Consulate accompanied by their White Russian mechanic. Both were heavily armed, for ever since his recent arrival in Urumchi it had been Greeson's devouring and as yet unsatisfied ambition to slay something, no matter what. Having been in the American Marines during the war he should have had enough of shooting and being shot at, but his eyes still lit up at the sight of a firearm, and to achieve his ambition no journey was too far and no labour too great. I think I felt much the same on first going to East Africa, but there one's blood lust could soon be sated whereas around Urumchi I saw no way of doing this short of manslaughter.

From here the road climbed more steeply through bald or scrub-covered hills which little prepared us for the startling beauty of the country immediately ahead. After topping a sort of pass (6000 ft.) we saw below us a great sheet of deepest sapphire water (15, 16), hemmed around by dark green pines, except on our side where a terrace of short grass dropped steeply to the water. Across the lake and above the pines shone the splendour of the new mountain world that we had come to seek.

In this glorious spot there is a Kazak village, and a monastery inhabited by Chinese Taoist monks; but to neither, picturesque and congruous though they no doubt were, did we pay any regard. Obviously the first thing to be done was to leap into that heavenly water—'the swimmer into cleanness plunging'—and the next to secure the boat, of which we had heard, for our passage across the lake. As became a Marine, Greeson charged himself with this task and he soon

(20) A Kazak trio riding into Urumchi past the wall which surrounds
the Chinese part of the town; the man on the left has a very fine piece
of headgear, the centre man wears what looks like 'a shocking bad
hat', and he on the right a mere Turki cap several sizes too small

(21) 'Pitched camp on the first convenient bit of scree a few hundred feet down;' the Schokalsky peak (*c.* 15,000 ft.) seen here is a fine mountain, not to be climbed easily

had a large, cranky, flat-bottomed craft (17) in perceptible motion. It was more than half full of water and when that had been baled out it filled up again rapidly. As a cargo boat it was useless so the ponies had to go round. We, however, who were not to be easily baulked of a day on the water, gaily embarked, stripped to the waist, and plied the oar—both oars, to be exact, but one was broken. More than an hour passed before we could sing the hymn:

> Now the labourer's task is o'er,
> Now upon the farther shore
> Lands the voyager at last

and I shall not be rating our oarsmanship too highly if I say that this lovely lake of Tien Shih is a mile long. Anyhow, we had beaten the ponies; and when, in concern at their long absence, we walked back to look for them and saw the nature of the track we understood why.

A little beyond the lake the wide valley we were following divided and a valley of almost equal size came in on our left. We had no guide, but our map seemed to show the route going up the left-hand valley. Shipton, whose judgment in these matters is usually better than mine, was certain the way lay straight on. The two streams seemed much of a size and neither looked like glacier water, although Shipton was equally certain that his stream drained the main Grachimailo glacier which he had seen from a distant hill on a previous visit. We took the left-hand valley which proved to be correct. A glance at the map will show how Shipton was deceived. Looking at the glacier from a distance no one would suspect that at its western end it drains *south* through a narrow gap between the main mountain and the Schokalsky peak, and that both our streams are cut off from the glacier by a low ridge not more than 12,000 ft. high.

The path now rose steeply until at about 8000 ft. we came to some Kazak yorts pitched on a steep grass shoulder where we camped (18). The Kazak are nomads or semi-nomads very like the Kirghiz of Kashgaria of whom they are a branch; but the intricacies of relationship between Kirghiz, Kazak, Cossack, Mongol, Tatar, the identity of the Great, the Middle, and the Lesser hordes, and such like, are conundrums only for students. There are said to be half a million Kazaks in north-east Sinkiang and about three million in the Soviet Republic of Kazakstan. The Ili revolt was a Kazak revolt, but those outside the province were still loyal to the Chinese who even saw fit to employ them as irregular troops in the bickering always in progress on the extremely vague Mongolian border. It was surprising that the Chinese trusted them so far (most of the Kazaks we met had arms of some kind): but on the whole they disliked them heartily because of their independent ways. This dislike was no doubt reciprocated by the Kazaks, so that the impression they gave us at our first meeting—that they were entirely opposed to strangers—was only natural. When we got to know them better they were friendly, hospitable, and helpful; but two encounters I had with them when alone and unannounced lead me to suppose that the Chinese dislike for them is no mere whim. On one occasion I was threatened with a rifle and on another with a whip.

These Bogdo Ola Kazaks do some cultivation in a haphazard way, whereas the Kirghiz of the west do none at all. They seemed poorer in livestock, and their yorts and furnishings meaner than those of the Kirghiz. Inside there were no decorated woollen bands securing the roof, whose outside also lacked the formal pattern and bright wool tassels often seen on the roof of a Kirghiz yort. Their aesthetic feelings, if any, seemed to find expression in wire-bound whips, ornamented saddlery, and above all in the men's hats. Their clothing was shabbily nondescript; anything served and served very well when set off by the proud hat the men liked to affect. These elaborate helmets (20) of lambskin rise to a high point and come down in flaps well below the ears; the outside may be a red or a bright patterned chintz quilted on, the whole trimmed with fur and topped with an elegant tuft of feathers. Thus crowned and well mounted, a Kazak appears to advantage; and their presence enlivens the drab streets of Urumchi where they resort for shopping (19). Like James Pigg they never get off, but leaning well into the open-fronted shop drive their bargains from the saddle.

That evening the 'Beg' arrived. He was the head-man of all the Kazaks on these northern slopes of Bogdo; his own yort, to which he conducted us next day, was higher up. From here Greeson had to return; which was a pity, because in the higher valleys ibex may be seen, and perhaps shot. Another of our party whom we should have been less sorry to lose was the Chinese policeman (mounted) who in spite of our protests had been detailed to accompany us. Whether the

Kazaks helped us on account of his presence or in spite of it was not clear, but we hoped that conditions higher up would overcome the scruples he had at leaving us.

The Beg's yort was in keeping with his position. Though perhaps not as fine as that of a Kirghiz Beg, it was well enough; the milk pans were impressively large—two or three feet across—and we had no criticism to make of the quality of the yoghourt. Lying on rugs in this spacious yort, sipping thin, slightly sour 'kumis' and sucking in spoonfuls of yoghourt, we felt much at ease. Unfortunately it was not yet midday, too early even by Himalayan standards to call it a day. 'Stretched on the rack of a too easy chair', we experienced some stirring of conscience and against our better judgment and against the inclination of every one else we pushed on.

Owing perhaps to our going so slowly or to the drowsiness induced by 'kumis', the familiar transition from juniper to grass, from grass to gravel, boulders, and finally snow, passed almost unnoticed. That we were getting high impressed itself upon us by the growing unwillingness of our followers, the yaks, the ponies, the guide, and especially the policeman. It began to rain and blow. We crossed the ridge at about 12,000 ft. and saw dimly below us a big, dry glacier, the Grachimailo. Thunder boomed. The rain turned to hail and then snow, so we hastily pitched camp on the first convenient bit of scree a few hundred feet down the other side. The men departed unreluctantly with their yaks and ponies, the policeman with very little persuasion followed them, and we four were left to contemplate what I thought a distasteful scene.

Our welcome to Bogdo Ola had been rude. Snow continued falling intermittently and the little of the mountain we were able to see gave us no pleasure. The main massif of Bogdo is a ridge (22) two miles long crowned by three upstanding peaks, the West, Central, and East, the last being the highest by several hundred feet. Apart from steep buttresses descending from the peaks the north face is a wall; both extremities of the ridge are cut off pretty abruptly, and there is no easy passage along the top from one peak to the next. That is to say that if one wanted to climb the highest peak, as of course we did, there was no getting at it from either of the other peaks or from the ridge between. It had to be climbed direct or not at all.

Between our camp and the mountain flowed the Grachimailo glacier, our camp lying opposite the west end of the ridge. Looking up
the glacier and across it to the East peak we could see the profile of a
steep rock arête descending from the peak. It looked attractively short,
exciting, and formidable and we decided that our first move must be to
have a closer look at it. Merzbacher's map (the survey was done by his
assistant Groeber)* credits the East peak with a height of 6512 metres
or 21,350 ft. To our weak minds such a height in such a northerly latitude—about that of N. Italy—seemed quite excessive. We preferred
the results found by a Swedish geological party, which had mapped
the region in 1932, which allotted to the East peak the more manage-
able height of 18,000 ft. We had learnt to our cost the previous year on
Muztagh Ata that latitude makes a big difference in temperatures and
snow conditions on high mountains; for in August we had experienced
there much colder conditions than we had ever done in the Eastern
Himalaya at similar heights. It disturbed us to see that so far our two
altimeters agreed closely with the heights on Merzbacher's map; but,
as will appear, we have reason to believe that his heights for the three
summits are 1000 metres too much. I have since had Merzbacher's and
Groeber's account translated, from which it appears that the heights
of the places he went to at the base of the mountain were calculated
from carefully controlled barometer and hypsometer readings, while
the heights of the peaks were ascertained by theodolite readings from
a measured base at Urumchi. The technical details will be found in a
note at the end of the chapter.

The Grachimailo glacier up which we walked next morning
afforded excellent going, at first on a surface of flat stones and then on
clean, dry ice. It is a unique glacier in my experience, for it drains in
two opposite directions. It is a sort of saddle-shaped glacier, the upper
eastern part draining to the north by a valley parallel to that by which
we had come, while the stream from the lower western half flows south
through a deep cleft between the West peak and the Schokalsky peak
(21) (c. 15,000 ft.). Our modest objective was a snow col on a low ridge
running north from the foot of the East peak; and we toiled up the

---

*   Dr Gottfried Merzbacher, an Austrian explorer who travelled in Central
Asia 1903–4.

(22) The Bogdo Ola group from the west; the summit on the right
edge of the picture is Schokalsky and beyond it, from right to left,
are the three peaks of the main massif, West, Central and East; the
low peak on the extreme left is the top of the 'broken rock ridge'
near the foot of the north-east arête

(23) The Grachimailo glacier is debris-covered in the foreground but presents a surface of clean dry ice higher up; on the left of the picture lies the low col to which we first went; to the right of it, capped by a cloud, is the higher col from which one would start for climbing the north-east arête—the black rocks rising from the col; between these two cols lies the broken rock ridge which we climbed on our second visit to the mountain

long easy névé slope towards it with our thoughts and eyes fixed on our goal and on the arête descending from it. Although we advanced but slowly, the aspect of the arête must have been continually altering, for it was curious how rapidly hope and fear, confidence and despair, succeeded each other. At first sight the arête had inspired admiration rather than apprehension. Its spare outline and simple directness appealed strongly to a climber's better and bolder instincts. But, as Dr Johnson says, 'there are charms made only for distant admiration—no spectacle is nobler than a blaze': as we drew nearer, the clean outline appeared to be marred by at least one abrupt step, while the general steepness aroused misgivings. There was no need to make any immediate decision as climbing was not possible until the recent snow had disappeared from the rocks.

On the far side of our col (c. 13,700 ft.) another glacier flowed from the bay between the arête and an eastwards extension of the main mountain, but this we could not well see on account of mist. There was some talk of descending to this glacier to have a closer look at this east ridge as a possible way up to the peak, but the silence which met this suggestion proved fatal. Unlike travelling in an aeroplane, when one crosses a col it is a case of what goes down must come up again; so this one-sided discussion ended by our climbing a short way northwards from the col. The slight gain in height we achieved would have given us a better view of the arête had not gathering cloud and mist shut it out. As we turned for home the storm broke.

Sleet, hail, and thunder continued for the rest of the day. 'Better is the end of a thing than the beginning thereof', saith the Preacher, and most mountaineers will cordially agree. They begin their day early to the accompaniment of broken bootlaces, a hasty meal, cold, darkness, and a rock-strewn path; and end it—a pious hope—by returning to a hut or a dry tent, a hot meal, or even a fire. Even if, as in the Himalaya it frequently happens, the return is to a wet sleeping bag in a dripping tent pitched on snow, there is nothing more delightful, except the reality, than the anticipation of lying in that wet bag grasping a pint mug of hot sweet tea in one hand, a spoon for the shovelling in of 'satu' in the other.

These delightful anticipations were not to be realised. Our leaking tent was by no means the only domestic calamity to be faced when we got home wet through. Given reasonable weather, with the wood we had brought, we should have been able to cook on a fire under the partly imaginary cover of a boulder. But the weather was most unreasonable, and Lakhpa, who like most Sherpas can perform prodigies of open-air cookery with wet wood in the rain, had now fallen sick. Hill Billy, slowly learning the routine of camp, was a comparative greenhorn and pretty useless. To call a man who spent his life travelling as a mail courier a greenhorn may seem severe; but most native travellers expect to find a house of some sort at night or at any rate a dry cave. If there is nothing at all, then they just don't travel that way. If by ill-luck they happen to find themselves spending a night out in conditions in which a fire and cooking are difficult, instead of persevering they fold themselves in whatever rags they have and sleep. Who sleeps, sups.

We were not so apt to take things lying down. Greed, or a spirited defiance of adverse conditions, compelled us to have a meal and a hot one at that. We must use the Primus, though it seemed wrong to use it with a load of wood lying by—a sentiment with which the Primus seemed to agree. Flames licked the roof of the tent singeing our hair on the way; pricker after pricker was bent, broken, and discarded; bonfires of matches and pints of methylated spirit were burnt in the priming pan, and the oil changed and rechanged to little purpose. Very soon the inside of the tent was a murky hell of soot, snow, mud, lit frequently by lurid imprecations.

At last we did coax the stove into giving us a hot meal and settled down in our wet sleeping bags to smoke and face the future—a mental exercise which by a curious association of ideas has become the last thing any of us cares to do. That Lakhpa would have to go down and that the Primus must be made to behave better in future were our first conclusions. But now that the arête was for the present out of the question, what were we to do next? The better to answer this question I reached for the map and failed to find it. Seeing me vainly groping Shipton began to grope in his kit, too; but this valuable aid to mountain navigation had been left behind, like the Dutchman's anchor, at the Kazak yorts.

He who knows not whither to go is in no hurry to move. The day broke fine and had we been in the habit of washing or shaving we

(24) This is on the east side of the lower col, where from the névé of
the glacier bay we looked up at the east ridge, part of which appears
in the upper right-hand corner of the picture; it is steep on this side
and defended by hanging ice and cornices

(25) The water from this tarn at the foot of the West peak falls over
the high rock shelf to drain southwards; in August the surface of the
tarn (*c.* 13,000 ft.) was mostly frozen; in the absence of yorts large
boulders such as these, by which to camp, are a powerful draw

should have made a leisurely toilet. We began, however, by moving camp to a larger boulder which promised more shelter for the fire. Then the policeman came up with a skinful of yoghourt and having attended to that we saw him off together with our sick man Lakhpa. In the afternoon we explored a route to the south. Crossing the snout of the glacier we dropped down the high terminal moraine to a desolate tarn still half covered with ice, putting up a couple of Brahminy duck from the water. On the shore we found pony tracks which we followed till we came upon a rough track and cairns on the lip of a big drop; for on leaving the lake the water tumbles over a rock shelf several hundred feet. At the foot of this the valley opened on to wide grass slopes and old river terraces. There were no trees, nor could we detect any signs of life.

We had seen enough to know that we could get ponies down the valley for we were already thinking of a move to the south, and in particular to the Chigo glacier to the south of the East peak. How far we should have to go down before being able to take animals across the ridge between we did not know, so before committing ourselves we went to have a look at the east ridge.

Next day (15 July) was fine. In two hours we reached the snow col, descended on the other side, and climbed an ice-fall to the glacier bay at the foot of the East peak (24). Fifteen hundred feet above us the ridge ran almost horizontally until it reared up to merge into the steep eastern buttress of the peak. The ridge looked possible and the buttress slightly less daunting than the arête; but on this side the approach to the ridge was guarded by hanging seracs so that the using of this route seemed to depend on our finding a way on to it from the south.

The assessing of risks of this kind is always difficult. Many factors have to be considered: the state of the snow or ice, night temperatures, how soon the sun will strike the offending seracs, how long the party will be directly under them, and whether any accompanying porters would think the mountain worth the risk. Most porters would, I think, offer only half-hearted approval. According to sound mountaineering practice risks of this kind should be avoided, and neglect of this rule is quickly followed by censure. On the other hand, by risking nothing, nothing can be gained. Most of us, no doubt, err on the side of caution. As Dr Johnson remarks: 'It can indeed raise no wonder that temerity has been generally censured; for it is one of the vices with which few can be charged, and which therefore great numbers are ready to condemn.'

MERZBACHER'S HEIGHTS

The altitude of each camp site was taken by readings of three Bohne's barometers of 10 cm. diameter every evening at 8 p.m. and every morning at 6 a.m. Observations were also taken with an Assman's aspiration-psychrometer and a minimum and maximum thermometer. These readings were controlled through observations of boiling-point thermometers which were made en route every other day. Besides this, at stations of several days' occupation they were checked by a diagram obtained from the Naudet barograph. During the march we used an aneroid barometer and at specially important points took boiling-point thermometer readings.

As there were no basic stations sufficiently near for the reduction of the barometer to sea level, the barometrical recordings taken during three days before leaving Urumchi were used as a check. For this period a correct mean height of the barometer was ascertained by using the observations made by Strokowsky over a period of three years in Urumchi. These calculations showed Urumchi to be 912 metres above sea level. The trustworthiness of the altitudes of the points climbed was further augmented by two control barometers kept at the main camp.

To ascertain the height and position of the peaks of the central group by means of trigonometry, a base of 791 metres was measured at Urumchi on a site twenty-three metres above the town on the west side. The instruments used were a Hildebrand theodolite and an invar tape which had been verified by Guilleaume in Paris. The calculations have been carried out at the Geodetic Institute in Munich. An accuracy of plus or minus thirty metres is claimed for the altitudes of the East peak, 6512 metres (21,164 ft.); Centre peak, 6501 metres (21,125 ft.); West peak, 6397 metres (20,787 ft.)

CHAPTER IV

BOGDO OLA: SOUTH SIDE

HAVING DITHERED FOR THREE DAYS, we now had to make a plan. Although the fine weather of the previous day had removed some of the new snow from the arête, its appearance still daunted us. The shock we had received by our first view would, we had assured ourselves, be lessened by a few days of exercise and acclimatization. We had had our exercise, we had had the arête under constant survey, and yet we shied at the notion of trying it except as a last resort.

We had a long discussion. There was the whole of the south side to look at, where unexplored and therefore comforting possibilities might lie. Shipton thought we should go there at once, since we had already wasted a lot of time. His opinion was that of Moses on another occasion: 'Ye have compassed this mountain long enough: turn you southward.' I was not so sure. Although the mountain is by no means vast—were it not for the uncrossable barrier of the east ridge one could walk round it in two short days—I felt that if we went south we should not return; and that before going we ought to rub our noses against the rocks of the arête if only to assure ourselves it was as bad as it looked.

At the subsequent enquiry held to decide whether our failure was owing to lack of competence, courage, judgment, or of all three, Shipton maintained that we should have done better to have made a wide preliminary reconnaissance of the mountain from all sides. Whereas I held the opinion that in the Himalaya a strategic reconnaissance of this kind is nearly useless because so few routes can be confidently approved or discarded without actual trial. Only a close reconnaissance is worth making, and unless the preliminary reconnaissance is very swift there is seldom time for both, and never time to give two routes a thorough trial. I think this is certainly true of a big mountain, even when two or three months are available; but, of course, much more can be learnt about a lesser mountain like Bogdo even in three weeks which was all we had at our disposal.

In the end, contrary to a well-tried maxim, we preferred the unknown evil and went south in the expectation of finding a route less exacting than the arête. We had sent for animals, but as we did not expect them till late I went on alone to reconnoitre. Having reached the cairns at the top of the big descent I at once noticed two or three flocks of sheep grazing up the valley. The knowledge that one is descending into an inhabited valley is usually welcome both to Europeans and their followers, implying, as it does, meat, milk, shelter, and possibly transport. Our Kazak followers were no doubt already aware of the fact, but for Shipton's benefit I scratched the glad tidings on a rock and sped on. At the bottom some horses were grazing, but the shepherds were still far away when I turned up the first likely looking valley to the east.

This is the valley into which the small Sud glacier between the West and Central peaks flows. The ridge at the head of the valley is thrown off from the Central peak but here it was quite low, without snow, and could be easily crossed. I went up to it by a loose scree slope and looked down on to the Chigo glacier which was the haven where we would be. I judged that the ridge ($c.$ 13,500 ft.) could be climbed by yaks, which was a big point. If we could have our loads carried up I was almost confident that neither of us would flinch from carrying them down the other side. True, we should have to bring them back, but by then they would be much lighter. On this flying reconnaissance of mine I thought I had made an even more important discovery in the form of a likely looking route to our peak. But my whereabouts were not so clear to me then as I imagined, clouds were down to about 16,000 ft., and I could not be sure. We found later that this peak up which I saw a way was only a 'false' peak and one a long way from the true East peak.

As it was now about 2 p.m. I hurried back to the main valley concerned to know whether the rest of the party had come down and gone on. Some Kazak women I met gathering yak dung merely looked surly; there was no sign of anyone having passed, nor any sign of movement up the valley. I started back and presently met a shepherd towing a sick sheep, accompanied by a nasty looking blackguard with a rifle. We had nothing to say, but I was sociable and sat patiently smoking a pipe while they looked through the wrong end of my field-glasses and

(26) 'We turned up the Sud glacier nallah and camped by the last
grass at about 11,300 ft.'; the snow ridge in the distance is part
of Schokalsky peak, and below is the deep valley into which we
dropped from the tarn; Merzbacher calls it the Gurgan Bogdo valley

(27) The south side of the east ridge proved to be much more acces-
sible than the north; from a camp on the rock island (centre) it took
two days to put a camp on the snow saddle; the ice on the lower part
of the slope can be easily distinguished; the Chigo glacier originates
in a big cirque behind the rock wall on the left

handled my ice-axe. Presently the armed gentleman indicated that he would like my shirt, so I got up to go. It wasn't a very good shirt, but it was the only one I had.

Being worried about the absence of the others I put on all steam up the valley and up the steep ascent to the cairns. Nearing them I heard a shout which I thought must be Shipton, but looking round I discovered the armed blackguard hot in pursuit either of me or my shirt. As I was near the top and he well down I had a good start; and a Kazak is better on a horse than on his feet. However, he was game. He topped the rise as I was approaching the lake several hundred yards away. But when I started climbing the moraine I saw he had sat down—not, I think in order to draw a bead but merely to draw breath. Ammunition, no doubt, was scarce.

I reached camp at 5 p.m. to find them just loading up and presently we got under way. With baggage animals the direct route was out of the question, so we had to fetch a long circuit which finally brought us to the lake from the other direction. There was a faint track, but it was hard to hold to it amongst the rocks. Several times animals fell and several times we had to go back to try a fresh line. It is astonishing how much ponies, and even yaks, dislike boulder-strewn track or hillside. Holding the beast's headrope one picks out what one thinks is an easy line and steps confidently over or between rocks only to find that the obstinate animal will have nothing to do with the carefully chosen way. At 7 p.m. we settled down for the night on the grassy margin of the tarn between two massive boulders (25). It was a good camp, and was heartily welcome to me, for I had had a long day.

Our animals picked their way gingerly down the steep zigzag path to the valley from where we turned up the Sud glacier nallah and camped by the last grass at about 11,300 ft. (26). On the way our pony men had made friends with the shepherds and later the son of the local Beg rode up to our camp with a present of yoghourt. We had this for supper mixed with puree of chilli to smarten it. Some foolish people—and, I'm afraid, most women— judge a dish by its colour, recoiling in disgust from peas, for example, or sprouts which have not been turned to a bright emerald with an almost lethal dose of soda. I feel sure that such misguided folk, although they probably would not have liked the taste of our dish, would certainly have applauded its artistic colour—the off-white of the yoghourt delicately marbled with salmon-pink veins of the purée oozing from a great bloodied gout in the centre.

Before taking a camp over the ridge we had to make sure that there was a way on to the east ridge of the mountain from the Chigo glacier. We told the Kazaks that we should probably want a couple of yaks to go as far as the ridge; meantime we held on to our original transport in order to remain strategically 'in balance'. The col on the ridge proved to be higher than I had imagined when I first climbed it, and the drop to the Chigo correspondingly long. There were but few stretches of 'runnable' scree, which in one way was a comfort. Obviously if one has to descend and re-ascend 1500 ft. of scree, as we had, the more exhilaration one has from scree-running on the way down, the more exasperating will be the plod up the same shifting surface. We crossed to the east side of the Chigo, which is a fine broad glacier, and sought for a vantage point from which to view the peak and the east ridge.

There was fortunately no doubt about our ability to climb the easy snow slope (27) which led from the head of the glacier to a nick on the east ridge; but as our eyes travelled along the ridge to the peak we began to wonder. Certainly, when seen from this side, the ridge looked longer, narrower, and altogether less adapted to the passage of a laden party. As for the peak itself, writhing mists prevented our seeing it steadily and seeing it whole. A short piece of snow rib momentarily seen would fill us with confidence, until a hole torn in the swirling vapours would reveal the rib springing out of nothing or ending in a horrid black cut-off. Obviously two camps would be needed—one at the nick and a second as far as possible on the further side of a deep gap.

We had much to ponder as we trudged homewards. The rolling, slow, rhythmic plod up scree, hands in pockets or folded behind the back, is conducive to deep cogitation or even to composition if one has a bent for it. Perhaps it was on some such slope that these sublime lines occurred to Joseph Cottle:

> How steep, how painful the ascent:
> It needs the evidence of close deduction
> To know that ever I shall gain the top.

(28) In the foreground is the rock 'island' on which we camped
before climbing to the ridge; the Chigo glacier, about half a mile
wide and two miles long, drains into the lake visible in the distance

(29) 'Next morning, carrying half-loads and treading hard snow, we
soon finished the climb to the ridge;' the ridge rises to a minor snow
summit before dropping to a deep gap; from the gap the snow and
rock rib running straight to the summit would have to be climbed;
its formidable aspect is better seen in (32) but this view which we had
on the way up was sufficiently convincing

On our return, Hill Billy, who had accompanied us on this walk, took to his bed. It was no doubt an unjust thought, but it did cross our minds that this sudden collapse had been brought on by the revolting aspect of the east ridge and the peak upon which we meditated assault. But he need not have had any cause for alarm either on his own behalf or on ours, for at that time temerity was the last vice with which we could be charged. Without assistance of any kind we were momentarily tethered, but as the next two days were wet and windy we were content to potter. We climbed a rock gully in pursuit of ram chikor—a very noble bird for the table—and paid a visit to the nearest yorts for tea and chat. They now agreed to let us have two yaks, and upon returning to camp we found Lakhpa had turned up. Prospects looked brighter, but so uncertain were we of the wisdom of this coming move that we now regretted our offhand rejection of the arête.

Hill Billy was left in charge while the three of us with two yaks and their driver started for the ridge at the head of the valley. At times we doubted if the animals would make it. The final bit was steep and loose and their feet were badly cut. However, by midday we were all on top. Here we left the yaks to browse a bit of gravel while we four bipeds went down with the loads. After brewing some tea at the bottom we sent the yak man back and continued up the glacier to a camp (c. 13,000 ft.) on some rocks at the foot of the snow slope (28). The Primus was at its tricks again and the three of us had to occupy a two-man tent; nevertheless, we had a fair night.

July 22 was a fine, hot day which proved to be the hardest we had yet had. The lower part of the slope turned out to be of rough ice upon which one felt very insecure without nick or rudimentary step to stand up on. Without a load one might have walked up it easily, but we soon found that with an unwieldy 40 lb. load on one's back it was extremely hard to use an axe, so that the leading man had to carve out a small stance for his load, cut ahead for a rope's length, and then come back for it. Thus occupied, I debated, without settling to my own satisfaction, whether we were caught in a bottleneck or in a vicious circle. Without loads there was no need for steps while with loads they were needed but could not be cut. The process was varied by the leading man hauling up all three loads, but it was no quicker and was not good for the loads.

Lakhpa made heavy weather of it. He was fat and he had not properly recovered from his recent illness, so at 3 p.m. we sent him down,
hoping but not believing that he might have time to recross the ridge
and get back to Hill Billy before dark. With three loads to handle Shipton and I struggled on till 5 p.m. when I for one was quite willing to
stop. Even then we were not clear of the ice, for there were still another
hundred feet or so. However it was pretty soft ice in which we soon
carved out a platform for the tent.

Next morning, carrying half-loads and treading hard snow (29),
we soon finished the climb to the ridge and returned for the rest. By
midday we had everything up and the tent and ropes spread out to dry
on a great rock that projected through the snow, as the previous day's
manoeuvres had thoroughly soaked them. On this brilliant morning,
climbing easily on firm snow, and not overladen, we had leisure to
look about us; and the higher we got the more we became convinced
that we had made a mistake. We could see now that the section of
the ridge between our camp and the mountain was no fit place along
which to carry a camp (32). It was long, knife-edged, and in places
heavily corniced. Moreover, the final climb of nearly 3000ft., where
the ridge stood up on end and leant against the peak, seemed to bristle with climbing problems well above the low standard of difficulty
we had set ourselves.

Although we were thus almost reconciled to defeat before we had
even completed the carry to the ridge, we had the resolution neither to
cut our losses and go down forthwith nor to persevere in an apparently
hopeless attempt. But had we gone down there and then we should
have lost much. Defeat had its compensations, for the site of our camp
was very grand; had we come up merely to enjoy the airy position and
the view we had not done amiss. To the north side of our ridge, where
the tent hung upon the very lip of space, the eye could range freely to
the black and gold wastes of the desert; from the tent door the slender,
glistening ridge stretched away to a hidden gap whence it leapt up to
merge with the precipitous rock and ice of the east face of the peak;
while to the south, beyond the broad white ribbon of the Chigo glacier
(34), the tawny Asian landscape seemed as infinite as the pale sky.

That night a violent wind blew. Our tent had been used on Everest
in 1938 so that considering its age and the fury of the gusts our surprise

that it held was equalled only by our gratitude. The night was clear and cold, stars blinked calmly, but even under this benign sky without any fierce accompaniment of thunder, lightning, or driving snow, the roar of the wind was terrifying. Against the walls of the abyss below the winds seemed to beat as if imprisoned, gyrating and bellowing in a swiftly rising crescendo of sound until at last they sprang out and burst over the ridge with a savage howl, plucking wildly at our frail shelter. The fabric flapped madly, the poles to which we clung groaned and bent, as the spent gust sobbed and moaned away across the snow. In the ensuing lull we lay with wan smiles and questioning eyes listening for the faint rumble which would herald the next onslaught. Prepared for the worst, we lay in our bags clothed in wind-proofs, helmets, and mitts, with boots ready to hand.

It cannot be laid down as a general rule for all high camps that joy cometh with the morning. The dawn may well be worse than the night, because there is no longer any excuse for lying still. Should one decide to continue lying, there is still the Primus to be lit. On this occasion, however, the rule held. Towards dawn the wind died and the dawn itself promised well. Without any debate or much compunction we turned our backs to the mountain and began climbing along the ridge in the opposite direction. The ridge seemed to continue for miles culminating at last in a snow peak very nearly as high as the main mountain. This was out of our reach, but we picked on an intermediate bump as our target for the day. It made a good snow ridge climb, with a bit of ice here and there, a cornice to add interest, until we at last achieved our modest summit (35). All this, too, in those conditions which are so desirable but, in the Himalaya, so rare—hard snow underfoot, and a warm sun overhead. What more could a mountaineer want than to climb easily along the bright crest of this high, untrodden ridge, where glittering slopes fell away on either hand to smooth snow bays; and to the wrinkled glaciers from which flowed rivers that must presently perish in the hot sands of Asia.

Is it, by the way, a sign of decadence, senility, or merely sanity thus to couple ease with enjoyment? I like to think it is sanity; for though on a difficult mountain one may experience many moments of 'fearful joy', the keenest pleasures of difficulty and danger are for most of us largely retrospective. Nevertheless, when, having achieved the summit of our modest ambition, we turned and allowed our eyes to dwell upon the sterner delights of the East peak we felt, like Macbeth, 'To be thus is nothing' (33, 36). Our felicity was far from perfect; and this is perhaps one of the wholesome merits of mountaineering, that there is nearly always some other mountain or route at hand to modify the raptures of the climber's success, prick his self-satisfaction, and fire his ambitions.

The height of this 'incident' on the ridge was about 16,550 ft. and our camp something over 15,000 ft. It was from these heights, which our altimeter gave and which our map confirmed, that we concluded that the East peak could not be much higher than 18,000 ft.

We were back in camp by 4 p.m., and so grand was our eyrie that we were in no hurry to quit. We expended much film in an attempt to record the light and shade cast on the snow by the sinking sun; and my confident assertion that the results would, as usual, be undistinguished led to a dispute about mountain photography and the difference, if any, between a competent and a beautiful photograph (31). Owing to our lack of theoretical knowledge the discussion assumed a personal aspect, slightly vitiated by the absence of any examples of our respective masterpieces. I think we were both prepared to waive the claim to ever having taken a beautiful photograph, but my declaration that I could not remember either of us having ever produced a competent one was hotly disputed by Shipton.

At this interesting point we were interrupted by a violent blast of wind, the precursor of another anxious night. With that prompt energy and decision which hitherto, when it was a question of going up, we had entirely lacked, we packed up and started down, carrying everything. When we came to the icy part we began to lower the loads rope's length by rope's length, until when near the bottom Shipton's impatience got the better of his judgment. We were not so near the bottom as all that. Our bulging rucksacks, cartwheeling and bounding madly, did stop at last, badly split, soaked in paraffin, and the lighter by the loss of several pounds of sugar. We retrieved them and carried them up to the old camp site in the dark. The Primus once again refused to burn so we supped drily on a crust of bread in profound silence. The rucksack episode seemed a likely topic for conversation, but it was one upon which only a very determined philosopher could have embarked dispassionately.

(30) 'The site of our camp was very grand'; to the right of the tent is a
precipitous drop to the glacier bay which we had previously visited;
the cornices are well marked; far below and to the left is the head of
the Chigo and the cirque; the friendly rock by the tent door made a
sun-warmed seat and drying-rack; had the tent been pitched below
the crest it would have been more sheltered, but that would have
involved a deal of hard digging to make a level platform

(31) This and the previous picture (30) are interesting because they were taken
just before the sun sank behind the East peak and we retired to our sleeping bags to discuss photography; I took a sombre view of our abilities, but
the two I had just taken would have spoilt my case, for they are better than
competent; the rude mechanic process of block-making has robbed them
of their bloom, dimmed their lights and weakened their shadows; in two
enlargements, made in a few minutes by an expert friend, the summit ridge
glows as if on fire, the rocks stand out blacker than ink, the snow sparkles as
if freshly fallen, and its texture is so evident that I feel like kicking steps in
it. In short, instead of being mere topographical keys, they are pictures that
provoke feeling and evoke memories

In the morning we carried everything down to some wood we had dumped at the bottom of the long scree slope and there we had breakfast. Leaving the tent to be brought up later we climbed to the ridge and got down to camp soon after 2 p.m. Hill Billy, who had now recovered, was dispatched for the tent while I set about making bread (37). Lakhpa had swapped his 'chapan'—a quilted gown, once maroon, now black with age—for a sheep, so that night we did ourselves well; better, in fact, than either of us felt we deserved.

The question now was what to do with our four remaining days. We had neither the time, paraffin, nor the inclination to go back and have a closer look at the north-east arête, whose summary condemnation we more and more regretted. There was the Schokalsky peak for which we just had time, or a lower but attractive looking isolated pinnacle above the yorts. We tossed up, and this Cairn peak, as we christened it, won.

Leaving the yorts at 5.30 a.m. we halted for breakfast on a snow shoulder just below what small difficulties the climb offered. And then, with Hill Billy tied inescapably between us, we mastered a short piece of ice and reached the top by easy rocks. Here Hill Billy built an immense cairn while we admired the tranquillity and subdued colours of a vast Asian landscape. It was an exceptional day, very fine, still, and warm; and an exceptional view-point. Besides the long south face of Bogdo (39) immediately behind us and another group of snow pinnacles further east, fifty or a hundred miles to the west rose peak upon peak of the great Tien Shan (38). Far below us the grass of a treeless valley dwindled away and died, swallowed up in the grey, gravel glacis beyond which, twenty miles away, lay the Urumchi road and the pale, reed-fringed Ainak lake. From this lake, according to local tradition, spring the fierce Turfan winds, one of which, no doubt, had tried to blow us off our ridge. 'All this wind', complained a dweller in the Turfan Depression, 'comes from a little lake on the way to Urumchi. There is an iron gate in the lake and it is only half-shut, if any one could shut it, the wind would stop.'*

Thus ended our first grapple with Bogdo Ola in which we had displayed little judgment and not much energy. We took horse next

---

*   Huntington's *Pulse of Asia.*

morning and after six hours bumping and jogging across the dismal gravel plain against a hot wind reached a small village by the lake. Although there was a telephone line, there was no telephone, so we spent the night in an inn and in the morning boarded the first Urumchi-bound lorry. We were back in time for breakfast at the Consulate where we met a warm welcome and many fresh faces.

(32) The tenuous nature of the ridge along which we had intended
to carry a camp as far as the gap is obvious; as are, too, the thorny
climbing problems with which the final 3000 ft. of rock and snow
seem to bristle; from here the north-east arête, which is the ridge on
the right, looks far from alluring; behind are the Central and West
peaks, and below the head of the Chigo

(33) A clearer picture of the north-east arête from our ridge camp;
given warm conditions, clean rocks, and a strong party it might go;
the high col and the top of the 'broken rock ridge' appear on the
right; they are easily attainable from the far side; heaven forbid that
they should have to be reached from this side

CHAPTER V

BOGDO OLA AGAIN

I N THEORY WE SHOULD HAVE STARTED next day for Kashgar by truck; but, as the driver might well have said; 'Alas, Sahib, it is but machinery.' The truck had been ailing before we left and the three weeks it had since spent in a Chinese workshop had quite undermined its constitution. The week of waiting that followed was trying enough for us. Every day some new ailment was discovered and towards the end the workshop closed down to allow the Turki and Tungan (Chinese Moslem) workmen to take part in the Moslem festival of Id.

It happened, too, to be a week of hot, cloudless weather and our ill-humour mounted daily as we watched the mountain and its northeast arête become more and more in good climbing condition. This touched a sore spot, for we had come back disgusted with ourselves for our lack of judgment and the pusillanimity which had stayed us. Except that they were strictly private, our talks concerning the conduct of the recent expedition resembled what is said to go on at conferences of Soviet officials, where each in turn methodically and ruthlessly examines his own shortcomings and consecrates himself afresh to mental and moral rearmament.

Since this was our frame of mind, it is not surprising that on the following Saturday afternoon we might have been seen throwing our belongings into an American truck about to start for the Sud glacier. The immediate impulse for this step came from the Pathan driver of our truck who had walked into the compound after lunch carrying a newly cracked piston which he thought we might like to see. How the American truck came to be standing by all ready to go, almost as if waiting to catch us as we reeled under this last and heaviest blow, needs some explanation. The fact that we had been at the yorts (40) within a few hours of a glacier the one day and in Urumchi the next, had made a strong impression at the Consulate. Always eager to promote interest in mountains we had pointed out that provided a truck was driven across the gravel glacis to the foot of the valley the journey to the yorts could be done in one day. This verdict clinched the matter so far as Greeson our former companion was concerned; all that remained was to obtain leave. In Urumchi, for the greater part of the year, the American passion for ice is catered for by an ice house. In August, however, this was empty; so at our instigation Greeson suggested filling it from the Sud glacier. A *modus operandi* was quickly sketched out and the Consul persuaded into allowing him to make a trial trip. Speed was the essence of the thing, and since he had command this was likely to be forthcoming.

Greeson rejoiced to be reinforced by us at the last moment, for in spite of our explanations his ideas of the geography of the place or even of the appearance of a glacier were a bit scattered. And not only our reputation but his chance of any future mountain holidays depended on his bringing back a substantial load of ice. Besides us two, Hill Billy and Lakhpa, there were the White Russian mechanic and his wife, an American girl visitor and an American journalist. All these piled into a jeep and a two-ton six-wheeler which already held an amount of gear in keeping with the urgency and importance of the expedition—arms, of course, in great quantity and variety, food and drink to correspond, tents and bedding, and an assortment of iron implements for carving up the glacier. These ranged from felling axes, bill hooks, pick-axes and crowbars to cross-cut saws. It was a pity we had neither explosives nor a glacier drill.

It was late afternoon before the convoy left the main road and began bumping slowly over the long gravel slope towards the foot-hills. Here the presence of parties of gazelle delayed progress, for Greeson seldom let us get past them without stopping for a shot. That this was done more by way of a salute than with malicious intent the gazelle seemed to recognise as they waited patiently until the fusillade subsided before bounding happily away. By nightfall we had reached the mouth of the valley. The truck could go no further, so here, where there were trees and where the stream had not yet disappeared under the gravel, we off-loaded our curious cargo and camped.

Overnight the weather broke, but this did not deter the eager Greeson who, accompanied by the mechanic who spoke Turki and Chinese, left for the yorts while the rest of us still slept. That they had

(34) Looking south down the Chigo glacier from the ridge; the foot
of the snow-free pass by which we came over from the Sud glacier is
about where the deep shadow lies athwart the glacier, a mile above
its snout

(35) 'A good snow ridge climb, with a bit of ice here and there, a cornice to add interest, until we at last achieved our modest summit'

found them was shown by the arrival in the afternoon of three camels. There were also a couple of ponies which we rode turn and turn about, for it was a steep grind up to the yorts which we did not reach until eight o'clock. The Beg was away, but his yort was crammed to capacity. Besides his family (41, 42), his son's family, and eight of us, a couple of Tungans turned up. They were on business, for it seemed they owned most of the sheep and goats which by now—milking time—were creating an uproar outside. The Kazaks told us too that for the most part they were merely the custodians of the yaks, ponies, and camels strewn up and down the valley.

The Tungans are the Mohammedans of China who observe most of the tenets of Islam. Their origin is obscure, but their more recent history is written ineradicably in blood; for they have rebelled fiercely and frequently against the Chinese both in Sinkiang and Kansu. Ruined towns and abandoned fields testify to the bitterness of these revolts and of their quelling. The Tungan is noted for commercial ability and enterprise as well as for his surly independence, which combines the business instincts of a Chinese with the aggressiveness of a fanatical Moslem. It is not surprising that he is disliked equally by his more easy-going Turki neighbours and by his Chinese masters.

In addition to preparing a meal, making bread, nursing babies, and milking goats, the women made tea for the men who had more important things to do or at least to talk about. In the absence of father the Beg's son did the honours—served the tea, led the prayers, and from time to time executed a strophe or two on a one-stringed instrument. The young man had a good deal on his hands; his Tungan visitors no doubt wanted an account of their sheep, we wanted transport, while Greeson, having relegated the getting of ice to its proper place in the scheme of things, wanted his company on a proposed ibex *battue* early next morning. This suggestion seemed unwelcome to our host, either out of regard for the ibex or for his duties as flockmaster to the Tungans; but a few swift words from his bustling young wife settled the matter. 'A wife's counsel is bad, but he who will not take it is mad.'

The weather had worsened considerably by next morning when the rest of us assembled for a late breakfast at which we calmly assessed the certain discomfort of the hunters who were long since upon the hill; for, as Mr Pecksniff rightly observed, 'if everyone were warm and well fed, we should lose the satisfaction of admiring the fortitude with which others bear cold and hunger'. According to plan the truck with its load of ice should have returned to Urumchi that day, but it was midday before Greeson turned up, wet through, without any trophy, but still cheerful, and two o'clock before the ice-cutting party started. In two hours we had reached the snout of the Sud glacier, having with us five yaks which were able to come very nearly to the ice (43). Each man chose his weapon and began a violent assault upon the watery, singularly impure ice of the glacier. The difficulty was to get chunks large enough to remain unmelted during the journey back. Even when one had got a good working face the stuff came away in bits instead of blocks, so that a piece of more than 10 lb. weight was a great prize. Filling the sacks was precious cold work, but soon all ten were filled, wrapped in straw to keep the ice cool, and loaded on the yaks.

By dusk we were back in triumph at the yorts where we had to spend another night, which was neither fair on the ice, the Kazaks, nor the American Consul. None of us, however, took this to heart, least of all the Kazaks who no doubt hoped that we were but the first of many equally rich parties of ice collectors. With the aid of some bottles of rice wine we made quite a night of it. We had few songs in common, but each nationality did its untuneful worst. An extravagant dance by the White Russian mechanic inflamed Hilly Billy to pirouette economically as they do in Hunza; and impelled one of the Kazak women (several months gone) to a merry and slightly unseemly dance popular in the high Altai.

The morning broke cold, wet, and windy. Shipton and I had long given up any hope of climbing the north-east arête—that prize, if it ever had been within our reach, was now snatched away. But we could at least go and look at it, so we seized upon two yaks and started up the valley, leaving the ice merchants to shift for themselves. We camped that evening by the tarn above the rock shelf near the foot of the Grachimailo glacier.

On another cold, windy morning we set out to reach if possible the high snow col at the foot of the arête, leaving the camp standing. Some six inches of snow now covered the dry ice of the glacier and the rocks of the ridge we had to climb. Below on our left lay the

(36) Having at length achieved the summit of our modest ambition
we allowed our eyes to dwell upon the sterner delights of the East
peak, and we felt, like Macbeth, 'to be thus is nothing'; In this picture the angle of the north-east arête (on the right) appears slightly
less daunting

(37) The master baker, whose unctuous, self-satisfied smile betokens the production of a sound loaf (balanced on the ice-axe) and not the achievement of some prodigious climb

approach to the low snow col we had crossed on the earlier trip, and on our right between us and the mountain itself was a steep narrow ice-fall. The ridge of loose rock which we were climbing terminated in a high gendarme overlooking the col we hoped to reach. It was a day of sunshine and storm, of wind squalls and scurries of sleet, and after climbing steadily for over three hours we were still several hundred feet below the col. But we were high enough to see sufficiently well the lower rocks of the north-east arête only two or three hundred yards away across the ice-fall (44). They were now well plastered with snow which was not likely to clear for several days, if at all, at this time of year. At this height and in this latitude I should doubt if much melting goes on after August. For what it was worth—for our judgment throughout the expedition had been palpably at fault—we recorded our opinion that the East peak might be climbed by this route by a strong party. It is less hazardous to suggest that it is not likely to be climbed by any other way.

The possibility that the Beg and his long-suffering family had by now seen enough of us may or may not have occurred to us; but anyway we decided to return to Urumchi by a new high level route. The spine of high ground from which Bogdo Ola rises like a dorsal fin descends gradually to the vicinity of Urumchi and then rises again further west where it merges into the main Tien Shan. In theory, having got on to the spinal ridge one could walk along it almost to the town, but in practice ridges are seldom so accommodating. Usually a ridge proves to be so broken that one must traverse below it, thereby crossing gullies innumerable or even whole valleys.

So it happened on this occasion. Having first outflanked the big Schokalsky peak we had to descend into and climb out of no less than four valleys. We were carrying our own loads, Shipton had sprained an ankle, and Lakhpa was not well, so that four times we were sorely tempted to forgo the anticipated pleasure of a ridge walk and to descend the valley in search of yorts and transport. In fact in two of the valleys we came upon yorts, and as the only fit man in the party it was my self-imposed and thankless task to steer my companions past them. In another valley we saw a herd of ibex grazing the lush grass like so many cattle. Ibex, like yaks, usually like their grass sparse and in fairly inaccessible places. We camped in the fourth valley where horses and camels were grazing but where the yorts, happily, were some way down. As we were still well above the tree-line we had to boil the tea on a yak dung fire, a process which took an hour. Dry yak dung makes an excellent fire with a pungent smelling smoke not unpleasant in small doses or at a distance, but wet dung, like green wood, is merely a hissing and an abomination.

Having cleared this valley we did at last attain the axis ridge to the west of the last snow peak. It was broad and smooth, and though we enjoyed our promenade for but a short time, the efforts we had made to reach it were well repaid. We experienced again the pleasure we had had on the Cairn peak. Normally the eye's range is so circumscribed that it seems to take peculiar pleasure in mere distance. Here hundreds of miles of Asia lay spread on either hand. There was nothing particularly to catch the eye, unless it was the Ainak lake, the only vivid piece of pattern and colour in a vast carpet of indefinite forms and subdued tones of opal, indigo, and old gold.

For five miles we proceeded thus easily, learning once more that it is not necessary to balance along a knife-edge ridge to feel the exhilaration of a vision of boundless space and breadth. Ahead the ridge grew less and less accommodating until, not far from Urumchi (which we could see), it plunged into a tangle of rocky hills and nallahs. On Lakhpa's earnest recommendation we committed our bodies to the depths of the first easy-looking valley to the north. In the upper part there was water, for which we were by then thankful, and at 9000 ft. the pines began, but it was rough going to the first yorts (45), which we came upon suddenly, pitched in a pleasant glade. We failed to impress the Kazaks with either our importance or our weariness. They gave us yoghourt but no horses. In order to explain ourselves we said we were walking to Urumchi for fun (46), to which the Kazaks coolly replied that in that case we might as well prolong our fun by walking for two more days until we reached Urumchi.

At the next yorts we met with the same treatment. It was late evening, Shipton and Lakhpa were both very willing to stop, but since we needed ponies to make sure of reaching Urumchi next day we determined to push on (47). What looked like a wheat field lower down the valley acted as a lure. Knowing the ways of these streams we might have foreseen that like the others the one we were following would

presently dive underneath the gravel. At about eight o'clock I reached
the field well ahead of the rest when I was immediately accosted by
two mounted Kazaks who first threatened me with a whip and then
tried to ride me down. While I was parrying the attack with an ice-
axe the others arrived and Lakhpa explained who we were. When they
told us that there was no water for three miles my companions were for
making a dry night of it, but in the end we agreed to go on until nightfall. Once more well in the van I met another Kazak, the first kindly
one I ever did meet when alone. We must dine and sleep with him at
his yort hard by; so while we waited for the others I helped myself to
the skin-bag of yoghourt attached to his saddle. No doubt it had been
dangling there all day so it was thoroughly well churned.

By ten o'clock we had reached the yorts where we dined on bread
and milk and slept in the open. Choosing a bed in the dark was difficult. It was essential to get well beyond the attentions of a multitude of
sheep and goats and the clear space upon which we eventually bedded
down turned out to be the main track. Early in the morning a party of
Kazaks thundered along it, their horses neatly avoiding our bodies.
Here we got three horses for the eighteen miles' ride to Urumchi. The
Kazak who came with us rode double with me most of the way. Probably he could have gone on for ever sitting a horse's hindquarters but I
found I could not, so I finished the last few miles on foot.

We arrived in time for a late lunch to find the usual number of itin-
erant Press correspondents who again impressed us with their ardour
in the pursuit of knowledge. One hoped, though hardly expected, that
their findings would be read with equal ardour. References to the ice
expedition, we noted, were avoided. That the party had been further
delayed on the way home had not told in their favour, and although
no less than 850 lb. of ice had been weighed in, the quality met with
criticism. While admirable for preserving tired fish or for applying to
the heads of delirious patients, it was found to be a trifle too gritty for
the ices and iced drinks with which Americans like to refrigerate their
stomachs.

Our truck was now ready for the road, but we had one or two serious engagements to fight on the Chinese food front before we were able
to disengage in tolerably good order, our heads aching but unbowed,
to begin the journey of a thousand miles to Kashgar.

Although I can hardly read without a tear the sublime descriptions of eating and drinking by such master hands as Dickens, Surtees, and, best of all, Peacock, there are no doubt many readers who, like Mr Woodhouse, love to have the cloth laid but are rather sorry to see anything put upon it. A description by any feebler hand of what is put upon the cloth may merely disgust, and is almost certain to sicken should the feeble hand attempt to describe what the Chinese put upon their cloth, where indeed it is often true to say, 'There's death in the pot'. It is curious and, I think, true that few readers will flinch at what is considered the more polite pastime of drinking, and none at all at references to love-making. In these respects readers are like Captain Wattle who was all for love and a little for the bottle.

The night before we left the Mayor of Urumchi gave us a farewell dinner party. Although upon these feasts the Chinese love to expend a deal of anxious thought, great gastronomic skill, and wads of paper money, it is not too much to say—and it is a very strong statement— that drinking plays almost as serious a part as eating. This, of course, is only as it should be, and the guest can only regret that the materials are such that they would be better poured into the sink than down the throat. He can, however, comfort himself with Sancho's reflection that 'cursed bad wine is better than Holy water'. But the Chinese value politeness even more than we do, and as the politeness they value most on these occasions rests chiefly in the guest refusing nothing, he had better save his honour by staying away should he feel that such a meal is likely to be a too severe trial.

I have read of a British consul who would attend these Chinese functions and sit through them in perfect silence neither eating nor drinking. Whether such a practice is regarded as a piece of sturdy British independence, abstemiousness worthy of a saint, or merely resolute and studied offensiveness, it is a feat rather to be admired than imitated. Certainly on this occasion this was Shipton's view, who made a point of taking things as they came and not infrequently taking them once again. Nor was I behind-hand in doing our host honour, so that in the end the example of Confucius, who stopped drinking just short of mental confusion, was forgotten.

(38) A vast Asian landscape seen from near the summit of Cairn peak; the snows of the Tien Shan are just visible in the distance

(39) The south side of the Bogdo massif seen from Cairn peak; the West peak is on the left; the Sud glacier is emerging from below the Central peak, to the right of which and behind is the much diminished East peak; our pass to the Chigo lies at the edge of the snow field on the right edge of the picture

CHAPTER VI

TO KASHGAR

THE TRUCK IN WHICH WE MADE this journey has already been the subject of some derogatory remarks but, in justice, it deserves honourable mention, for it was the sole survivor of the two 30-cwt. Fords which Sir Eric Teichman drove from Peking to Kashgar in the autumn of 1935 (48). Even at that not very distant date, motoring in these parts was in the pioneer stage, so that such a journey reflected much credit on the truck and on its occupants. Since those days, the truck had been constantly in use, seldom on metalled roads, and had been to Urumchi and back more than once. During the war the road to China across the desert and through the Kansu corridor had received some attention to facilitate the trickling flow of Russian aid to China, and at the same time the Kashgar road had been re-aligned and in places remade. Nothing had been done to this road since, and now its pot-holes and corrugations were to give this veteran truck yet one more shattering experience.

The driving throughout was shared by Shipton and the Pathan driver Mir Hamza. Out of what I took to be consideration for my nerves or mistrust of them I was allowed to enjoy the purgatory of the spare seat in the cab. Mir Hamza was a fine figure of a Pathan, tall, lithe, bearded, rather temperamental, and addicted to enterprises of a most private kind. When we reached Kashgar, he found that his wife had been thrown into prison on a charge of opium smuggling; and it was as difficult for the court as it was for us to believe in the husband's protested ignorance of the ways of the viper he had so long nourished in his bosom. It was an episode embarrassing both to him and to his employer, and one which it was extremely difficult to laugh off.

He was a good but careless driver—in fact completely carefree so far as anyone else on the road was concerned—a hard-hitting mechanic, not without some intimate knowledge of his own vehicle. He had with him a Turki assistant, a fellow Moslem, but as meek and insignificant

as he himself was proud and over-bearing. He only performed the
onerous but menial duties of filling up with water and petrol, but his
life was made a burden to him by the Pathan. Between them, however,
they could change a tyre with noteworthy *élan*.

The Kashgar road follows the Turfan road as far as Davanchin
before branching west to Toksun. Beyond Toksun the road enters the
Subashi gorge (where it becomes mixed up with and indistinguishable
from the river bed) through which it climbs for the best part of 3000 ft.
to the Argai Bulaq pass. One gorge is very like another. They vary only
in depth, narrowness, and starkness; but a pedestrian is much more
likely to be overwhelmed and oppressed by them than is the motorist
whose passage is but brief and whose mind is absorbed by the perils
and difficulties which such a road provides. In this Subashi gorge,
however, there was little danger of meeting oncoming traffic and none
at all of going off the road to hurtle to death in the river below; for the
road remained in that safest of places, the bottom, so that one drove
among the sands and boulders of a perfectly dry river bed. After halt-
ing at dark, we could find no water with which to brew tea, and we
were by no means sorry to start again at 3 a.m.; when a waning moon
had transformed the rather dreary rock trench into a sculptured clois-
ter of silver and ebony.

I walked most of the way up to the pass; and such was the nature
of the road that there was little danger of being over-hauled. We
dropped down from the pass through strangely chromatic hills of
ochre and black to Kumush, where there is little else but a spring.
Here we broke our fast and our thirst. Thus fortified, we embarked
upon the hundred-odd miles to Karashahr where we were to spend
the night at the Chinese yamen. Even if I could remember the scenery
I should hesitate to describe it; for a mountaineer must agree with
Ruskin that mountains are the beginning and the end of all scenery.
Here the mountains were far off, and even if one takes a less exclusive
view of what constitutes scenery it is difficult for anyone, who is not
a Doughty or a Lawrence, to say anything fervid, or even kind, about
desert or near-desert.

Whether a passenger as distinct from a traveller has any call to be
interested in the passing scene is questionable. The driver of a vehicle
certainly has not and by choosing that mode of travel his passengers

(40) Looking back to the West peak from our camp close to the yorts in the Gurgan Bogdo valley; the camel looks a bit 'ribby' and is without the thick hair, particularly the tufts on the thighs, which make some of these beasts appear enormous—a poor specimen of its kind

(41) A Kazak family; father and mother in the middle are flanked by son and daughter-in-law; the latter's small daughter wears a number of silver dollars

have clearly indicated that their interest begins only at the destination, and the way there is a tedious interlude best passed in sleep. I have not often experienced it but I imagine that sitting in a cinema is much the same as a journey by car, in that both are as it were negative experiences. One looks at the screen or out of the window (on both of which it is probably raining) to an unfamiliar scene with which one has no concern. The scenery or the story unfolds rather rapidly, carrying one by places at which one might wish to pause, if only for elucidation, and lingering or stopping at those which can hardly be passed too quickly. As the journey or the film comes to an end the senses begin to function again; and all that has passed might never have been. The eyes have seen but the brain has wisely refused to receive an impression too blurred to be accurate, too inconsequent for reason, and happily too slight to be recalled.

As we approached Karashahr we found that haze shut out any view of the great Bagrash Kul. From this lake comes a fine carp-like fish, while on its shores are bred the famous Karashahr ponies, the breed to which, according to Lattimore, we should look rather than to the Badakshan for the true Macedonian strain. We ate the fish of Bagrash Kul that night, but on this journey, alas, we were more concerned with broken springs, worn-out tyres, and petrol, than with the points of some Bucephalus.

The river which flows through the town rises in the Yulduz valley of the Tien Shan and flows into the lake. It was the finest river I had yet seen, wide, deep, fast-flowing, and of a clear steely blue colour; and yet in a short distance this living, dashing torrent dwindles to a trickle and dies in the sand, an end which awaits all the rivers of Kashgaria. But for few of them is this a matter of regret; except in winter most of them are some absurd colour—brown, red, yellow—wherein no really edible fish will live and no fastidious man will care to bathe.

As became passengers, we were hell-bent for Kashgar and had no time to waste on Karashahr (49), the Black City, with its mushrooms and melons, its ponies and fish, and bazaars where Kazak, Tungan, and Turki jostle and chaffer. We arrived late and we left early for Kucha, 180 miles distant. Beyond the pleasant oasis of Korla there are a hundred miles of semi-desert. It is not true desert, for the soil is loess and supports occasional wild poplars and tamarisks. The latter, growing out of huge mounds of earth from fifteen to fifty feet high, are characteristic of this country, and according to Huntington, indicate climatic changes:

> ...one finds the tamarisk mound in every stage of development from one foot high with a vigorous growth of bushes, to sixty feet high with nothing but huge gnarled trunks, dead for hundreds of years. On flood-plains from which the water has been diverted for four or five years half the tamarisks are usually dead. In later stages still more die, and only those with very deep roots persist. Then the wind begins to dissect the plain, carrying away the finer materials and heaping up the coarser grains of sand in the protected spots where living bushes check its force. Thus mounds are formed and their height is increased by aeolian erosion at the base and aeolian deposition at the top. The depth to which erosion can proceed is limited by the level of underground water, and the deposition by the amount of sand available from surrounding areas. The actual size of mounds depends partly on the length of time since the water was withdrawn. I should say that mounds fifty to sixty feet high must be nearly two thousand years old...

We stopped some seventeen miles short of Kucha (50), an ancient and celebrated town, one of Turkestan's Six Cities, where the girls are reputed to be 'all like flowers'. This failure, however, did not deter us from rising again at 3 a.m. for the third morning running to cover an equally long distance to Aqsu. However much one dislikes motor travel, I should dislike travelling this road by any other means, unless perhaps in a faster car or on some winged steed 'fretting to roam the desert'. A few weeks in a horse-drawn cart, for example, would soon pall, even though the road is enlivened by tamarisk mounds. But from Bai, which is about half-way, we saw some real scenery—the Tien Shan. There had been a gale in the night which had swept the sky clear of loess dust and far to the north above the dun plain rose the silvery slopes and white towers upon which a mountaineer can never look without a sudden urge of joy. Whether we could see Khan Tengri (23,620 ft.) the highest of the Tien Shan we could not say. Khan Tengri has long been accepted as the highest, but our Russian friends have bedevilled this as they have done so much else by asserting that they have discovered a higher.

Whether the following account, from a Russian source, of this discovery is correct or not, it is interesting for its refreshingly immodest style. Nevertheless, the survey of the Tien Shan by Merzbacher in 1904, was fairly thorough, and the discovery of a mountain 1500 ft. higher than Khan Tengri only about ten miles away is remarkable to say the least. The following report made by V. Ratsek, a member of the 1946 Tien Shan expedition, may be of interest:

The knot of mountains lying due east of the Soviet Tien Shan have for a long time attracted the attention of explorers. Here, surmounting passes hidden beyond the clouds, bypassing roaring rivers and gigantic glaciers, went expeditions whose work tore asunder the veil which hitherto had kept the secret of Nature concealed from Science. Until recent years the current opinion was that Khan Tengri, the principal summit of the Tien Shan, was the highest peak in Russia. The alpinists conquering the Saryjas range observed in the south-east only clouds covering the peaks of the Kokshal Tau [Khan Tengri lies here]. Thick banks of cloud perpetually lay on snowcovered ledges. Travellers considered the mists over the Kokshal Tau as a regular phenomenon. Members of the 1940 expedition, however, managed to get a glimpse of the summits of the range from the Saryjas pass. These peaks clearly surpassed the Khan Tengri in altitude which, however, could not be finally determined as the explorers did not have the necessary precise geodetic instruments; neither had they the benefit of the important preparatory exploration of the Military Topographic Department carried out in 1943. Surveys made by that expedition ascertained that about 16 kms. south of the Khan Tengri on the upper regions of the Zvezdochka glacier there towers another gigantic pear-shaped ice wall. This peak of 7440 metres (24,180 ft.) is not only the principal summit of the Kokshal Tau but is the highest point of the whole Tien Shan. The Khan Tengri 6995 m (22,730 ft.) hitherto regarded as the highest of sky-piercing mountains should thus stand aside and give up its right to pre-eminence. The 7440 m. peak discovered in 1943 is the principal summit and not the Khan Tengri. This summit was discovered and its height determined in the phase of our patriotic war when our victory over the enemy was a foregone conclusion. That is why this gigantic summit, the second in altitude in the U.S.S.R., should serve as a monument to our great victories and bear the proud name of Victory Peak.

One feels sorry for Khan Tengri thus triumphantly diminished to the greater glory of Soviet topographers who have also lopped it of a thousand feet. According to 'Burrard and Hayden' its height is 23,620 ft. which V. Ratsek reduces to 22,730 ft. The highest peak in the U.S.S.R., to which this new Victory Peak (Pik Pobedy) comes second, is what the Russians call Stalin Peak, 24,590 ft., climbed by M. Abalakov in 1933; the large party, of which he was one, approached the peak by way of the Fedchenko glacier, forty-eight miles long, the longest in Asia. This peak, listed by Burrard and Hayden as Garmo, is in the Trans Alai at the junction of 'Peter the Great Range' and that of the 'Academy of Sciences'; thus, judging by this name, in the U.S.S.R. mountaineering and science are honourably married and not in illicit liaison as they are with us.

In the article from which the above is an extract there is a lively account of the post-war activities of Soviet 'Alpinists'—scaling cloud-splitting summits, planting the Red flag in what have unfortunately proved to be not inaccessible places, and generally tearing asunder Nature's veil for the benefit of Soviet science. In fact they have been doing a great deal more high mountaineering than we have, even if they have done it to a jarringly loud accompaniment. Nature by now must be getting used to having her veil torn, and will, no doubt, continue to smile, or sometimes frown, upon the scientists busy in what Goethe called their charnel-house.

We reached Aqsu (51) at 7 p.m. on the fourth day out from Urumchi. There we spent a whole day, a break which we had well earned, but it proved to be of such social activity that I found it almost as benumbing as counting tamarisk mounds. At Aqsu there is a large garrison and we spent our time at the barracks as guests of the Brigade Commander who was a friend of Shipton's. On the first evening we dined in the Mess in simple, soldierly fashion. We enjoyed the meal, but our hosts apologised for it, and threatened at the same time to treat us to a European dinner before we left. My heart sank. There is nothing so dangerous

(42) Mother and daughter-in-law inside their yort; even in these close quarters there seemed to be an entire absence of friction and the consequent angry sparks customary in this relationship; Lakhpa (with wrist-watch) is blowing up the yak-dung fire

(43) The snout of the Sud glacier to which we took the yaks to load
ice; it looks clean enough but like most glacier ice it was com-
pounded largely of grit and gravel

as a cook who meddles with foreign affairs; and this threat, which was amply fulfilled, hung over me all next day as we grappled with our successive gastronomic problems. The company at Mess was remarkable for its preponderance of generals and colonels who themselves were remarkable for their youth—Chinese subalterns, one imagines, very properly take their meals in the nursery. The whole atmosphere partook of that youthful fervour which the Kuomintang has long since outgrown. Smoking, drinking, and the use of imported luxuries were frowned upon or even forbidden, and the walls were hung with elevating texts. Moral re-armament was, rather belatedly, in full swing.

The Chinese are not great hands at breakfast. This is perhaps not surprising for most of their favourite foods would greatly astonish a dormant stomach. However, that did not prevent their sitting us down in front of a great bowl of rice and seeing that we ate it. Too soon after that the scene shifted to a pleasant villa on the outskirts of the town where we immediately began lunch with a General Li and his wife. General Li, as the commander of the garrison, was a man to whom the rules of moral re-armament either did not or could not apply. Austerity is all very well, as the General profoundly remarked, but it does not suit everybody. It was not one of those long drawn-out affairs of many courses beloved of Chinese officials, but there were a great many good things put on the table at once amongst which one could browse and experiment like a bee passing from flower to flower in search of the true nectar. Perhaps if I had to award the palm it would be to the bamboo shoots stewed in syrup, though the less exotic mince dumplings with a good dollop of soya bean sauce were not far behind. We finished with a famous blend of Hangchow tea with chrysanthemum petals floating in it—perhaps the 'Precious Thunder Tea' we read of in Marco Polo. The flavour was so delicate as to be imperceptible.

This luncheon party was a sort of training meet for the real business of the day. This was a garden party given by a Turki who was in official jargon the Administrative Superintendent— in unofficial jargon the 'big cheese'. This had little in common with the tepid, top-hatted ordeal that an English garden party appears to be. True it took place outside, but the only evidence of a garden was a tired zinnia and a rampant vine, under which the guests were firmly seated instead of being allowed to stroll about to meet and avoid friends. Though the vine was

a magnificent widespreading thing like Jack's beanstalk, laden with
grapes, it could hardly be expected to cast its ample shade over the
whole multitude. The host, a loose Falstaffian figure in flowing robes,
sat with a few exalted guests, like the Chinese generals and ourselves,
behind a long table in the grateful dappled shade; beyond the table, at
a respectful distance and on the earth, squatted the remainder of Aqsu
in tight circles of which the outer rows basked or sweated in a pitiless sun. There is nothing easier to bear than the discomfort of others;
indeed, this was a refinement that gave us added pleasure as we sipped
our tea and cracked our melon seeds in coolest ease.

When we arrived the company was being entertained, or more
correctly entertaining itself; but those at the high table might partake
of tea, melon seeds, and conversation in order to mitigate the ordeal.
It is, perhaps, true, that few amateur entertainments need be given
undivided attention, but this was well worth watching. No man and
very few girls showed any reluctance when called upon to do a turn.
They could all dance and sing, gracefully and pleasingly, but rather
too incessantly, either in groups or singly. There was a man, a hunch-
back, who laughed—a performance which nowadays, as one can well
understand, is heard only on gramophone records—and finally Aqsu's
woman delegate to the Urumchi assembly of Collective Wisdom, home
for a visit to her constituency, was called upon for a dance. She performed very capably but concluded with a short and powerful appeal
to patriotic fervour.

All the Aqsu girls were graceful and many of them comely. Even
those with more unfortunate faces looked well enough with their black
hair falling in long plaits adorned with black silk tassels, embroidered
velvet caps perched jauntily on their heads, many-hued satin waist-
coats, and equally vivid skirts. Beside these birds of paradise the men,
some in seedy European suits, looked commonplace, but they danced
and sang with no less grace. They moved stiffly but with much graceful
arm-work to a band of two guitars and a tambourine; when each dancer
considered he had done enough he took station opposite some fellow
guest and danced there until the victim obliged by taking the floor.

Meantime at the high table more serious matters were being
attended to. From pecking at melon seeds—a despicable chicken-feed,
in my opinion—we had progressed to green and purple grapes, the

(44) The north-east arête as it appeared from the 'broken rock ridge' after three days of bad weather; the snow col from which the climb would start is just visible on the left edge; with the rocks in this condition the climb is not on

(45) The first yorts pitched in a pleasant glade surrounded by spruce;
this yort is mean and shabby, like its owner, who refused us ponies
and advised us to keep on walking

bloom still on them, piled high on brass trays; water melons—messy and flavourless; real melons—food for angels; apricots, and roseate, fleshy peaches. Then came great discs of hot, rich-golden Turki bread into which I sunk my teeth pretty freely, defying the threatened European dinner and unaware that this was merely the harbinger of the coming storm. Greed struggled with dismay when a sumptuous platter of pastry and mutton was planked down in front of me with the intimation that there was plenty more where that came from. Here was no child's play, no finicking chop-stick work, no knife-and-fork cut-and-thrust, but a bitter hand-to-mouth struggle. I set to work manfully. The pastry was crisp and melting, the meat fell juicily from the bone at a touch, but no sooner had greed triumphed without much difficulty over dismay than our brigadier gave the signal to go. How I hated that austere man. Usually I am of the opinion of Mr Woodhouse that the sooner every party breaks up the better, but on this occasion I was never so reluctant to leave in all my life—to have snatched from me that 'rich and gigantic vision of the higher gluttony'.

We had warned our generous Chinese host that we must take the road again that evening, but they were not to be denied the pleasure of confronting us with a European dinner as a mark of their esteem and as a salutary warning to themselves. Apart from the Garrison Commander's lunch and my short but severe onslaught on the mutton and pastry we had been pecking at some trifle or other most of the afternoon. But there was no escape. At five o'clock we had not only to eat but appear to enjoy eating a slightly distorted version of a European meal which might have been intended either for breakfast or dinner, but which was in fact a mixture of both. The *hors d'œuvre* were in their rightful but always unnecessary place, as were the fish, meat and game which remorselessly followed; but then we were startled and very nearly subdued by bacon and eggs, slightly cheered by the appearance of pancakes, staggered afresh by soup, dumbfounded by hard-boiled eggs, and palsied by an ice.

We left at 6.30 p.m. and at 9 p.m. we camped. Beyond Aqsu all is desert; and that night as I lay upon its slightly heaving surface a Chinese general in an embroidered cap danced across it eating chrysanthemum petals with a wooden spoon.

After another long day in which we covered about 180 miles we had to spend yet another night on the road some fifty miles short of Kashgar. An average speed of more than 10 m.p.h. on this Urumchi-Kashgar road is good going. Evidently, after the road had been re-aligned and drained under the spur of war, it had been handed over to Providence for care and maintenance; this is an arrangement that works well on surprisingly few occasions, but is the easiest to make for a road through uninhabited country. A solution satisfactory to every-body except to the troops would have been to remove them from the towns where they were kicking their heels to employment on the road; but the 'brutal soldiery' seldom appreciate what is good for them, and, except in war-time, must be handled carefully.

The country through which the road runs is not completely unin-habited. Gazelle thrive in spite of the rifle fire to which they are sub-jected from passing lorries. Mir Hamza, by luck or marksmanship, slew two which had foolishly lingered within 200 yards of the road. He dropped them dead with two shots, a feat which reminded me of that friend of mine in East Africa who killed two elephant with one shot. The first beast, feeding on the edge of a steep-sided donga or wadi (we are momentarily in Africa), on being hit, fell and broke the back of the second which was feeding in the dry river bed below.

Next morning our hard-used truck, festooned with haunches of venison and the Consul's flag, delivered us safely at Chini Bagh in time for a second breakfast. Chini Bagh, the residence of British Consuls since 1890 and a port of call for Central Asian travellers both distin-guished and undistinguished, was now nearing its end as such. It was to be handed over to representatives of Pakistan and India and Ship-ton awaited only the arrival of the newly appointed Indian Consul before hauling down the Union Jack and quitting Kashgar for good.

CHAPTER VII

CHAKAR AGHIL RECONNAISSANCE

———————◆———————

THE MOTIVES WHICH HAD IMPELLED us to transfer ourselves so swiftly from Urumchi to Kashgar were mixed. As Shipton had been absent for more than two months from his office it seemed just possible that a letter or even a telegram requiring an answer might be waiting for him, while my chief concern was the advancing season (it was now September) and the need to act quickly if we were to attempt another climb.

In spite of this urgency I spent a week at the Consulate wrapped in sensual but perfectly proper delights, 'till languor suffering on the rack of bliss, confess that man was never meant for this'. The only exercise we took was a ride of some ten to twelve miles before breakfast and as this seldom took more than an hour it was fairly violent exercise, at any rate for the horse. Since my visit of the previous year and the death of Shipton's borrowed steed on the Ulugh Art pass he had acquired one of his own. This bright bay was no 'pampered jade of Asia', at least not in that brief early hour when we pounded out of the town along the red, dusty road scattering the incoming tide of donkeys, splashed through the shallow river like speed-boats, and charged along the country lanes and through the narrow alleys of outlying villages. Like Jorrocks, neither of us was afraid of the pace so long as there was no leaping.

This picture of flying hooves and wind-tossed manes had to be slightly modified if one was not mounted on the fiery bay. My mount had to be chosen from the stable of post-horses used for carrying the mails from Kashgar to Tashkurghan. As I learnt later, when I did the same journey mounted on one, these stocky animals could amble along all day under a load with a man sitting on top without noticing it; but they were not the fleetest of their kind. Though they may have been bred on the high Pamir amongst the Kirghiz, they could never have swept across Asia and half Europe as did their ancestors with the Golden Horde, and had they made the attempt they would certainly have arrived too late for the capture and sack of Budapest. They lacked spirit, they were immune to the contagion of speed which is enough to set most horses alight and will sometimes make even a donkey cut capers. The few that were not immune and gallantly strove to match the flying bay were so crippled by their efforts that I was never allowed to ride the same horse twice.

The doctor, who was also vice-consul, having held the fort for so long, was in need of a change and he therefore decided to come with me on a reconnaissance of Chakar Aghil, a 22,000 ft. mountain upon which Shipton and I had had our eyes for some time. In fact it had figured upon our programme of the previous year, but our plans had been upset by the Muztagh Ata episode. The day before we started we lunched at the Russian consulate as we had in 1947. I calculated in the interim that M. Bikmozin had done four days' work, for the business consequent on the receipt and dispatch of the Russian mail was a quarterly affair. This quite ample interval was owing to the broken bridges on the Andijan motor road which the Chinese authorities preferred should remain broken. A truck, I gathered, could do the journey, but as it had to be hoisted bodily across rivers three months' preparation and thought were none too much. I suggested to M. Bikmozin that he should use an amphibian truck to which he replied with his own particular brand of humour that such a vehicle savoured too much of militarism for so civil a man as a Russian consul to use.

Nevertheless he was neither sinking under the fatigue of this brisk correspondence nor comatose with boredom. For he was about to be relieved from what he no doubt thought the living death of Kashgar and was accordingly sprightly, congratulating Shipton on his approaching release and at the same time condoling with him at the demise of the British consulate. Our entertainment differed in no way from the first occasion except that this time I suspected the vodka of being watered, for I drank a great many glasses without beneficial effect of any kind. A straw shows which way the wind blows, but whether this frugality indicated the coming economic collapse of Russia or treachery on the part of M. Bikmozin's butler I could not decide.

The doctor and I went by truck to the road end on the bank of the Gez river some twenty-five miles west of Kashgar. Mir Hamza, whose wife was still a guest of the police, drove vindictively, giving

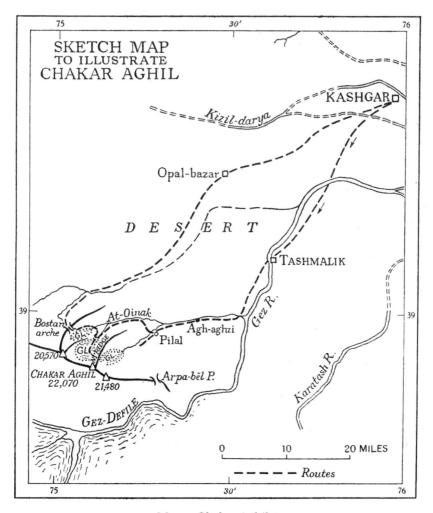

Map 3: Chakar Aghil

the donkey traffic even shorter shrift than usual. On emerging from the mountains where it runs through a difficult defile the river spreads itself over several hundred yards of gravel and sand and thus becomes fordable. The mount I had borrowed for the passage foundered in mid-river where it sank belly-deep in sand, depositing me in the water. Our destination was Tashmalik, about fifteen miles away at the edge of the foothills where our baggage had already gone by bullock cart. The doctor rode a borrowed horse—what J.J. would have called 'a hugly beast' if ever there was one—while I walked. The sight of a horse is said to make the traveller lame, but in my opinion much depends on the horse. I am a little nice in the matter and provided the way is neither long nor across absolute desert I find it less trying to walk than to be carried at walking pace on the kind of nag commonly allotted to the borrower or hirer of horseflesh. In walking one soon attains a soothing state of non-self, a sort of Buddhist trance, impossible to a rider whose mount, sensing the rider's condition, either takes the wrong way or in its turn adopts the Taoist principle of dealing with less and less until it finally arrives at inaction.

Strolling thus through poplar-shaded lanes or across short sun-bleached stretches of desert we arrived towards evening at the oasis of Tashmalik and made our way to the house of the Beg. The Beg, or headman, of a large oasis like Tashmalik is a considerable figure, whose household is likely to be run on lines agreeable to his dignity and with whom it is therefore desirable to lodge. The doctor had already had some professional dealings with the Beg's son so we dumped our gear on a veranda in his courtyard and sat there in happy expectancy. We sat for so long on the carpet of hope smoking the pipe of expectancy that I began to fear that the doctor's professional attention to the son had had ill or even fatal effect, but at last some slaves arrived bearing tea, a plentiful supply of melons, and apologies for the Beg's absence, and at ten o'clock expectation was fully realised with the serving of a rich pilau—'chau fan', as the Chinese call it, 'rice that is grabbed with the hands'.

In these regions food is provided freely, but transport either grudgingly or not at all. It was late in the morning before we were mobile. The animals reluctantly given were to accompany us only to the next village three miles away where we were assured we should

(46) The sight of all these horses made the travellers lamer than they
already were; nevertheless we had to continue walking

(47) Prolonging our fun, according to the Kazaks' advice, through
delightful but very dry country; the trees diminish in size as the
altitude gets less

easily find transport to take us to the mountains. After two hours of pleading, wrangling, and some show of violence on the part of the Beg's man who came with us, we got away from there with two woebegone ponies and a donkey. This gallant little beast had the task of leading the two horses over the Gez river which had to be crossed again by a less easy ford than the first. If by some unhappy chance a murrain were to carry off the donkey population of Sinkiang, the whole economy of the country would be at an end. Without them the women, the greybeards, indeed, most of the manhood, would be anchored to their homes; upon them depends all the day-to-day carrying of wood and water for the people of the oases, while upon the extended journeys of the traders it is the ass which leads the long string of camels and which shows the way across rivers to animals twice as big as itself. For these services the only rubbing they get is with an oak towel and the only food chaff into which a grain or two of barley may have inadvertently strayed.

By a good track we followed the left bank of the river. The foothills were now close at hand, but still gave no hint of the mighty Kungur range rising just behind them. Towards seven o'clock we reached the junction of the Oitagh Jilga, a river fed by the glaciers of Chakar Aghil. The camping ground lay on the other side and at this hour of the day the river was well up. Having had much experience of fords I find that my preparations for crossing them take an increasingly long time—the unlacing of boots and securing them round the neck, the rolling up or removal of shorts and the emptying of pockets—and I have an uneasy feeling that this deliberation is in the hope that someone else will be ready to take the water first. Unluckily on this occasion it was the inexperienced doctor who was ready first and who before I could stop him stepped light-heartedly into the flood and was at once in difficulties. Having no visible means of support, that is without ice-axe or stick, his legs crumpled under him, the boots which he was carrying were let go, and after being unceremoniously rolled over two or three times he crawled out on the further shore considerably battered and with the loss of those useful articles. But it's an ill wind that blows nobody good; I found I had left behind all my socks except for a thin pair I wore with rubbers, and to fill the gap thus left in my climbing boots I was now able to borrow from the doctor, whose 'chaplis'—the only footwear he had left—required none.

Our route now became more exciting. The warm red rock and the eroded yellow loess walls of our new valley were terribly gaunt, but high above them was the dark green of pines and faint behind them floated a white mass, detached as a cloud, which could be no other than Chakar Aghil. Some seven miles on, after climbing to a sort of hanging valley, we came to the golden wheat-fields, square mud houses, peach trees and poplars of Agh Aghzi (54). Still higher the valley forks, the left branch descending from the Arpa Bel pass (13,000 ft.) and the glaciers draping the north-east side of Chakar Aghil, and the right branch, the At Oinak, draining the glacier system to the north-west. It was the watershed between these two systems, the north ridge of Chakar Aghil, which we wished to see. In a previous visit Shipton had been up towards the Arpa Bel from which side the north ridge of the mountain appeared inaccessible, so that by going up the At Oinak we hoped to find a way on to the ridge from the north-west.

Half a mile above the junction, up the left branch, is the village of Pilal where we camped. It was not much out of our way, for near the village is a bridge and the track to the At Oinak. Pilal village is graced by a noble plane tree which put the reedy poplars to shame. Most of its inhabitants were up at their summer grazings where they live in yorts like Kirghiz, though they themselves are 'Taghliks' or mountain-dwelling Turkis. Its height is about 7000 ft. I climbed another thousand feet to where some stunted juniper grew. From here I could see up the valley the first of the pines and the wrinkled snout of a great glacier, but the clouds were low, the weather thick, and promising to become worse.

Having crossed the main stream by the bridge we followed a rapidly deteriorating track up the narrowing valley of the At Oinak. Apart from some camels grazing by the river there was no sign of life. A few miles up, the track quitted what had now become a gorge to turn unexpectedly up a side nallah of insignificant size. It seemed to lead nowhere, but presently the track climbed abruptly out of it to land us upon a wide plateau of short grass well above the gorge. In the distance, tucked away at the foot of pine-clad slopes, we saw some yorts for which we made at full speed like homing pigeons (55). Whether it

(48) The 30-cwt. truck, sole survivor of two which Sir Eric Teichman drove from Peking to Kashgar, where it became the property
of the Consulate; the Consular Union Jack is displayed by the near
side lamp; this Peking-Kashgar journey is described in *Geog. Journ.*
vol. 89 (April 1937)

(49) Karashahr is a market for wool brought down from the Yulduz
region of the Tien Shan pastures north of the town; this wool-laden
cart drawn by three horses harnessed abreast has very high, well
dished wheels

is seen at the end of a long day or at the beginning of one, a yort is the traveller's lode-stone. If it occurs in the middle of a march, as here, then it is a temptation to stop and I for one am not overfond of resisting temptation. The inhabitants were true Kirghiz whom we trusted were as pleased to see us as we were to see them. Anyhow we made ourselves at home, graciously accepted tea, and set the women to work making bread. Once they had got over the suspicion that we were tax collectors the neighbours began dribbling in, and when the doctor's profession had been bruited about 'House Full' notices had to be put up.

We were now at about 9000 ft. but cut off by trees from any view up the valley. Above the yorts on the north side was a high bare ridge which looked a likely viewpoint and as it was advisable to see something before making a plan for the next day I decided to climb it. The day was still young, and the doctor, having seen the last of his patients, wanted to come with me. As he had only chaplis for his feet I did not encourage him, but he was determined to come. This stout leather sandal with thick, nailed sole is the footwear par excellence of the North-West Frontier, where there are undoubtedly hills which chapli-shod tribesmen undoubtedly climb—and pretty nimbly, too, I gather. But on other hills, or on unpractised feet, the chapli is a form of foot-gear which neither I nor any wearer I have seen could or would use for long. This heretical view was amply confirmed that afternoon at the expense of the doctor. Having cut his feet and bruised his ankles by the stones and brambles on the way up, he found that as soon as the slope steepened his heels were more often out than in. When crossing difficult places he had to take them off, for there is no guarantee or even likelihood that one's foot will remain in the same place as the chapli.

I made matters worse by picking a direct but very bad route up steep unstable rock and across hard gravel slides where one had to scrape steps. But I had to retreat in some fear for the safety of my companion. However, by five o'clock we reached the ridge at about 13,000 ft., the determined doctor with lacerated feet and socks, and with the supreme footwear for hillmen dangling from his waist. Although the clouds were down to 14,000 ft. we saw something of value; below us lay a glacier-filled valley, the right moraine of the glacier being flanked by wide grass flats on which grazed yaks and scattered sheep.

The next day was the last we could spare for reconnaissance, so that it behoved me to get as far up this glacier as I could. The doctor's feet, very nearly beyond repair, urgently required his own professional attention, so I went alone. The cloud which for the last few days had covered the mountains and which had no doubt deposited much snow had now lifted, so I started early in anxious haste to get as high as I could before they closed down again. A mile up, the valley divided again and at the point of junction the snouts of two glaciers converged. The path turned up the left-hand valley climbing to the moraine of the glacier flowing in from the north upon which we had looked the previous evening. Just round the corner were two yorts. I passed these unnoticed and sped across the grass flats below the moraine.

A couple of miles of good flat going brought me level with the foot of the first ice-fall where the glacier tumbled over a steep step. From a shale shoulder above the step, at about 12,000 ft., I paused to take stock. The glacier, very crevassed and broken, extended more gently upwards and then divided into three great bays of névé. The bay in which I was interested lay out of sight round a corner to the left so I started traversing upwards across steep shale slopes thereby cutting off a good slice of the corner. Above me on the left was an extraordinary peak of perpendicular faces and right-angled cut-offs which I called the Geometry peak (56). Beyond the corner, between the glacier and the shale slopes, a snow slope lying at an easy angle afforded excellent going until at a height of 14,000 ft., having come far enough, I sat down on a rock to puzzle things out. An unexpected sight, even though unwelcome, may have charm. Indeed, that eminent critic Mr Gall decided that in the laying out of pleasure grounds unexpectedness and beauty were equally necessary ingredients, although, as someone unkindly pointed out, the charm of the unexpected cannot be exerted more than once. Here I had expected to find the scene dominated by Chakar Aghil, but whoever had laid out this pleasure ground had taken pains to disguise that notable peak. A magnificent ridge of snow and ice stretched in a great halfcircle around the glacier head and its several bays. It ran almost horizontally at about 19,000 ft. except where it shot up to two peaks of over 21,000 ft. neither of which looked in the least like Chakar Aghil. Moreover, they were too far west to be visible from the Oitagh valley as Chakar Aghil had been. Up in the corner of the left-hand bay the snow upon which I stood appeared to continue unbroken until it met the extremity of the cirque, and some way west of the point of junction was a rather insignificant snow bump. The sky was curiously dead, the light too feeble to cast shadows, so that it was impossible to say whether the bump stood on the cirque or stood back from it. Anyhow it could hardly be Chakar Aghil. And where on earth was that considerable protuberance of 22,000 ft.? If it was the first out-standing peak westwards along the cirque, then it would be the devil of a long climb, especially if we had first to traverse the bump. Certain of nothing except that what must be the north ridge could be reached, I went down.

On the way back, from the village Pilal, we had a view of Chakar Aghil which was quite the best we had had and which increased my bewilderment. It looked like nothing I had seen from the north-west side, so although my report of the mountain's elusiveness might make Shipton laugh it would hardly encourage him to come and climb it. We camped at Agh Aghzi under some willows in a garden whose owner took pleasure in giving. Eggs we might expect, but he pressed upon us melons brought all the way from Tashmalik. It is too cold for them at Aghzi, but the donkeys which take to Tashmalik charcoal burnt in the higher valleys return with loads of melons.

We met with another example of Turki kindness when early next morning we rode down to the Oitagh Jilga ford. A party of traders were breakfasting there, one of whom at once started up and ran across to us with a plate of sliced melon and bread. While most Central Asian trav-ellers have something disparaging to say of the Turki character, few fail to remark on their kindly disposition, a quality which a casual traveller will instantly discover and appreciate, while his other virtues and vices go unsung or unrebuked because unnoticed. Fortunately unanimity of opinion is still fairly rare in the present world and one well-known Central Asian traveller, Col. Schomberg, feels obliged to record that 'the Turki will never entertain anyone unless compelled... There are exceptions, but, generally, in a land where food is particularly cheap and abundant, true hospitality is as rare as true morality.' Ellsworth Huntington, in his *Pulse of Asia*, lists the Turki's qualities as follows:

among the good 'are gentleness, good temper, hospitality, courtesy, patience, contentment, democracy, religious tolerance, and industry; among the bad are timidity, dishonesty, stupidity, provincialism, childishness, lack of initiative, lack of curiosity, indifference to suffering, and immorality'. But Burke long ago pointed out the difficulty of drawing up an indictment against a whole people, and so, I think, the traveller had best refrain from generalising about the moral qualities of a whole people, but content himself with heartily damning or praising those of the individuals he meets.

As if to point this moral we were presently able to acquit some Turkis at any rate of that lack of initiative which Ellsworth Huntington charitably ascribed to them all. At Tashmalik we changed transport for the last time, leaving that pleasant oasis with two horses (both lame) and a donkey. Sitting by the bank of the Gez ford was a gang of semi-naked loafers who from time to time could turn an honest penny by giving a hand to bullock carts which frequently got into trouble in mid-stream. In crossing a wide ford local knowledge is everything, and these worthies very obligingly volunteered detailed sailing directions which, when followed, quickly sunk us in the deepest part of the river. Whereupon, the horse having lain down and the donkey floating away, the loafers with a whoop of joy dashed to our assistance, carried the stuff across, and reaped the reward of their enterprise.

The faithful Mir Hamza who was waiting for us quickly drove us back to the Consulate. He seemed more cheerful, for he was once more enjoying the society of his wife, justice having been tempered with mercy or with something more tangible.

(50) Kucha is a town inhabited wholly by Turkis and unvisited by
Kirghiz and Kazak or any other hybrids or nomads; it is one of the
Six Cities (which are in fact oases) of Turkestan, the others being
Korla, Aqsu, Kashgar, Yarkand and Khotan

(51) The open air market at Aqsu with awnings trimmed to the sun;
without the patient ass in the foreground, and the rest of his tribe,
there would be no market days in Aqsu or anywhere else, for upon
them the whole economy of Kashgaria turns

CHAPTER VIII

CHAKAR AGHIL

———◆———

T HE LESS SUCCESSFUL A MISSION the more reason there is to wrap its lame conclusions in a cloud of verbiage. My report on the chances of climbing Chakar Aghil by the north ridge was neither lucid nor conclusive, in fact, as we have seen, I was not at all sure I had been looking at the right mountain.

Having cleared a space at Shipton's office table by sweeping to the floor piles of those dreary, cheap brown paper files affected by Indian Government offices, we sat down to sketch on the backs of official telegrams our representative ideas of the Chakar Aghil massif, its ridges, glaciers, and valleys. The map of the region is content with indicating roughly some high ground. Shipton therefore based his map on what he thought he would have seen on his previous visit if the mountain had not been in the way, while I drew what I actually had seen on a day when the mountain wasn't there. Shipton's, I think, was the more credible. This was to be expected as it was in accord with the latest philosophic teaching whereby the evidence of one's eyes is of little value compared with the results of pure reason and higher mathematics. Anyhow, from our combined efforts it rather looked as though the mountain had no west side, or that if it had the glacier there had no outlet. But I hastened to point out, as we picked up, perhaps unnecessarily, the files, that conclusions which are drawn logically from unsound premises must of necessity be erroneous. We decided to have a go.

Two days later, 11 Sept., we loaded the truck and started once more for Tashmalik. Instead of Lakhpa we took his brother, Gyalgen. He was without Lakhpa's great belly, but also lacked his experience, intelligence, and drive. That, of course, is a negative description, and since Lakhpa's intelligence was of no mean order it would be truer to say that his brother had none at all. In addition we took a long, lean, cadaverous Kirghiz of grave aspect. Had his fine features and habitually grave

expression been set off by a well trimmed beard instead of a few straggling wisps he would have resembled my notion of a Spanish Don. On
several occasions the Don had been out with Shipton on some big-
gish hills after *Ovis poli* and had so astonished him by the prodigious
speed with which he moved up, down, or across difficult ground, that
he, Shipton, concluded that upon Chakar Aghil the Don would hardly
draw short breath.

We reached Tashmalik that same evening where the Beg put as
bright a face on the matter as he could. Three visits from me in ten
days were a little hard. But having a full-blown Consul on his hands
instead of a mere Vice he bestirred himself over the transport to such
purpose that we got away pretty early. Before leaving, we climbed to
the flat roof of the house whence we had a grand view of our mountain.
The day before we left Kashgar there had been a prolonged and violent
storm of wind and dust which had swept the sky so effectively that
even at that great distance the snow upon the mountain fairly spar-
kled. The north ridge, which we could see well, looked a likely route,
but why this outstanding summit had not been visible from the west
side was still unexplained.

Crossing the Oitagh Jilga in the early afternoon we pushed on
to Agh Aghzi where we camped in the same willow-hung field. And
on the third day, sternly ignoring the proffered entertainment at the
first yorts, we rounded the corner and took up our quarters at the two
rather mean yorts close by the glacier. There are not many towns in
Asia, or Europe either for that matter, so pleasant as Kashgar, and
there are fewer still from which within three days one can reach the
foot of a 22,000 ft. mountain. Gilgit is one and Chitral another; both
very pleasant, but hardly towns in the sense that Kashgar is. This two-
yort valley, we were told, is the Kichik Chi. There is no timber, only a
little juniper bush, but with the long wall of 'eagle-baffling mountains'
at the head and the wide grassy maidan at its foot it is a valley in which
men might well live a hard life and yet exult in living.

True to the principle of the economy of force we took a pony to
the far end of the maidan and as far up the shale slope at the side of
the ice-fall as we could. The application of this principle is one that
the wise mountaineer fully understands, especially in the Himalaya
where, unlike the Alps, opportunities for practising it readily present

(52) The centre of the town and the mosque, Kashgar; the picture
was evidently taken on one of the few days in the year when no
market is held; normally this open space is ringed with stalls and
thickly thronged with humanity, through which even a laden ass can
scarcely cleave a furrow

(53) The hat market, Kashgar; the normal Turki headgear is the little embroidered cap which the man on the left in top-boots and frock coat is wearing; the man next to him has on a black velvet job similar to those displayed on the wall to the left; the white hats on the right-hand rack are of dressed skin trimmed with wool and may be for winter wear

themselves. In short there is nearly always some man or brute beast to carry one's load. And since at the moment of writing I have not to practise what I preach, I may safely deplore that this should be so. As long as such reliable porters as Sherpas are available there cannot be the compelling incentive of necessity, which otherwise would before now have obliged the mountaineer to improve his own carrying power by studying the technique of load-carrying; and to lighten his equipment, both by the use of new materials and by elimination of much that is still held to be necessary. It might urge him to consider, for example, the use of snow holes instead of tents, so that it should become normal practice for peaks up to, say, 23,000 ft., to be climbed without porters, whose cost in wages and clothing is a severe drain on the resources of small parties. (On the north-east spur of Kangchenjunga in 1929 the Bavarians used an ice-cave at 21,600 ft. and thought it warmer than a tent.)

From the earliest day of Himalayan travel and mountaineering porters have of necessity been employed to reach the mountains or to cross passes, but their use for carrying camps up a mountain is a comparatively recent innovation. General Bruce first thought that Gurkhas might be useful in this respect; and in 1894, in order to test them, Conway climbed with two Gurkhas in the Alps. In 1895 Mummery and his two Gurkhas were killed while crossing a pass on the north-east side of Nanga Parbat. Nevertheless, before the first world war the most usual practice for Himalayan mountaineers was to take Alpine guides. In 1905 Longstaff with the Brocherel brothers (Italian guides) reached a height of 24,000 ft. on Gurla Mandhata (25,350 ft.) when, by the way, they camped at 23,000 ft. in a snowhole; and in 1907, accompanied by the Brocherels and a Gurkha, he climbed Trisul (23,360 ft.) from a camp at 17,500 ft., so that on the actual climb the party carried nothing at all. However, after the first attempt on Everest in 1922 the capabilities of the Sherpa porter became fully realised. Their employment in putting camps high on a mountain saved a great deal of sweat, and, as compared with Alpine guides, a great deal of money. Since then their use has become normal practice both on the great mountains where they are really needed as well as on the lesser where they might be dispensed with. Thus, in my opinion, their discovery and use may have led to the abandoning of earlier, simpler, and harder methods, and thus to slowing down the progress of Himalayan climbing in general.

If any such stern line of reasoning presented itself it was very quickly suppressed as we dejectedly acknowledged that our pony could be taken no further and that our backs could no longer escape their share of the load. Traversing across the shale slope carrying loads would have been so laborious that we stuck to the glacier trough where the way lay partly on dirty, black ice, partly on moraine, and in one place up a river of mud sliding slowly down the underlying ice. Although it is often the best way and sometimes the only way up a steep glacier, this trough where the ice of a glacier rubs against the mountain is always extremely rough and has a dismal air of dank decay from which one is always glad to escape. When we reached the corner and came to the foot of the same snow slope which I had struck higher up we found that the snow of a week ago had gone, leaving bare a bed of old, dirty semi-ice. We climbed easily up this and at four o'clock pitched the tents at my highest point. Our altimeter made this 14,400 ft. and a hypsometer reading gave 13,600 ft. All the snow had gone, so that we lay warmly on gravel, and this disappearance of the fresh snow combined with the brightness of the day gave to everything a different aspect. My continuous snow slope to the ridge was found to be broken by an intervening glacier, and my contemptible snow bump, which we now saw stood well back from the cirque, was no other than the distant and very noble summit of Chakar Aghil.

The discovery of this inconvenient break in the snow slope gave me some uneasiness, for the principal inducement which I had held out to Shipton to come had been this supposedly certain way to the north ridge. That evening I went up another 800 ft. and satisfied myself that the route would still go. At 6 p.m. a sharp fall of temperature to below freezing-point augured well for the morrow.

With our sad experience on Muztagh Ata the previous year still fresh in our minds we were in no doubt as to the necessity of having two camps, one at 17,000 ft. and the other at 20,000 ft. For this we should have a total load of about 100 lb. to carry. For some reason, about which I am not yet clear, this calculation was based upon a decision to take only one tent and therefore only one porter. Had we taken both tents and both porters our individual loads would certainly have been no more, probably a little less. But we make so many stupid mistakes in the course of an expedition, a climb, or from day to day, that unless the consequences are painful to pocket, person, or pride, our reasons for making them are seldom analysed. Should, however, an attempted analysis fail to disclose the wherefore, then one may at any rate congratulate oneself on not being reason's servile slave. If we had a reason for our odd decision, it was, perhaps, because boots, bedding, or warm clothing were insufficient for both Gyalgen and the Kirghiz. Anyhow, the fiat went forth that only one victim was required and unhappily the lot fell on the Don.

Shrinking from the ugly thought of having to assume our full burdens so early in the day we roped in Gyalgen, so that when we started he and the Don carried the bulk of the stuff between them. The route went very neatly. Our slope quickly narrowed to a ridge which took us up to the intervening glacier at the one point at which it could be reached. Immediately to our right it tumbled in a steep ice-fall to the main glacier bay below, and to our left rose a high rock wall. Having got on to the glacier by an ice bridge we walked across to a broken ice-wall on the far side up which we climbed with only a little step-cutting. This move landed us fairly on a smooth unbroken slope running easily up to the foot of the north ridge. Here we divided the loads more or less equally amongst the three of us and sent Gyalgen down with instruction to go to the yorts taking with him the spare tent.

Up to this point a slow slug would have had no difficulty in keeping up with our two porters, particularly the Kirghiz. We attributed this to their loads and refrained from comment, which must always come ungracefully from the unladen man. When we started again, the Kirghiz had no more weight on his back but he soon began to lag. The slope was easy and un-crevassed, there was no need for the rope, so we plodded on while the Don dropped further and further behind;

> And slow howe'er my marches be,
> I shall at last sit down by thee.

One began to doubt it.

Towards evening we reached a snug snow hollow, a hundred feet or so below the crest of the ridge, where we decided to camp, the height being about 17,000 ft. Dumping our loads we went down several hundred feet to the Don who by now had almost ceased to struggle, and relieving him of his load we got him up to the tent. He seemed to be very ill, spitting, coughing, groaning incessantly, and refusing all food. We ourselves had a very curious dish of Vienna sausages which were sizzling hot at one end and frozen hard at the other—a striking example of the non-conductivity of sausages in high altitudes. It is an original way of serving them which I cannot recommend.

Few indeed are those high camps where the inmates at one time or another are not 'acquainted with sad misery, as the tann'd galley-slave is with his oar'; and the misery is particularly poignant when one sleeps, as we did, three in a two-man tent. It blew hard in the night which I spent cold and restless, to wake, or rather sit up at last, with a fierce head-ache. Shipton, who is usually more at home in high places than elsewhere, greeted the unwelcome dawn with some muttered comparison between the worth of the game and the candle, while the cadaverous Kirghiz was in a thoroughly poor way. He had eaten nothing and had spent the night only semi-recumbent, moaning and spitting, until he at length became a total wreck.

The implications of this were obvious. Even if we were sufficiently callous to leave him there alone we could not go on because we had only the one tent. Brought up in comfortable homes and with a background of more or less comfortable mountaineering neither of us proposed going on to sleep in a snowhole at 20,000 ft.; or of attempting the climb from where we were; or, perhaps best of all, leaving the Don in a snowhole. By no means this last, for the unhappy man now alarmed us by beginning to spit blood. There was no question but that we must take him down; and since Gyalgen had removed the other tent ours must go down too. In short Chakar Aghil had beaten us.

A cold but fine, sunny morning served to deepen our chagrin, but before packing up we climbed to the ridge and a little way along it for the sake of photography. This ridge in no way resembled that of Bogdo Ola; on its comfortably broad back we could see no great obstacles between us and the distant summit. The long cirque or semicircular ridge, whose gigantic scale we could now appreciate, filled the whole western horizon like the flood-lit facade of some giant's palace as the rising sun kindled its rock buttresses to a warm glow and its two high bastions to pyramids of fire. On the east our ridge overhung a broad snow plateau upon which the slanting rays of the sun etched an intricate pattern among the seams and terraces of the crevasses. Many

(54) Part of the village of Agh Aghzi in the Oitagh Jilga; the village
is, of course, irrigated, for without water the flat on which the village stands would be as barren as the conglomerate cliffs above it;
although the rainfall is slight the cliffs are deeply eroded

(55) 'In the distance, tucked away at the foot of pine-clad slopes, we saw some yorts for which we made at full speed like homing pigeons;' the baggage train, seen here, has to approach more sedately; Hill Billy, heavily armed, brings up the rear; out on the left with a rifle slung across his back is the inevitable policeman

thousands of feet below lay the Oitagh valley, still in cold shadow, where a grey glacier crept down to the sombre pines (57).

We had now to rid ourselves of our sorrowing incubus who was well-nigh helpless. Most of the descent he accomplished in a sitting position held by the rope, and when we reached the little glacier where such effortless progress was not possible he was just able to stand up and stagger. At the 14,000 ft. camp site we put up the tent and left him with some food for a recovery squad to bring in; while we, a little too readily perhaps, responded to the call of the fleshpots at the yorts.

The case of this Kirghiz was so striking and the results so lamentable that at Kashgar we had him medically examined. For what it was worth, for in Kashgar such an examination could be only superficial, it showed him to be in normal health. Yet here was a man who had lived his life at about 10,000 ft., who danced like a flame upon his own mountains provided they were not much higher, and yet collapsed completely at 17,000 ft. In 1947 another Kirghiz, who in the course of a brief morning climbed to about 16,500 ft. on Muztagh Ata, also became ill— severely ill judging by his groans—but he was not, like our Don, a picked man who had shown a superlative aptitude for running up and down hills. Two men are not a fair sample, but one is tempted to conclude that mere living at 10,000 ft., as most Kirghiz do, does not increase the body's toleration to greater heights.

While Gyalgen went up to retrieve the Kirghiz Shipton and I turned our hands to 'shikar'. That is to say, Shipton carried a gun and I acted presumably as the 'tiffin coolie' without whom the thing is on a pretty low plane. Our quarry was the ram chikor, a big, fat, juicy, partridge-like bird, marked like the small chikor, but because he lives on or near the snow-line has much more white about him. We poked about, gradually gaining height, until we saw some ram chikor planing down to settle on a ridge above us. The birds generally feed uphill so our object was to get on to the ridge below them and stalk them until either we got a shot or they took fright and zoomed off the ridge. Pursued in this way the ram chikor is a very sporting bird; for although you have every intention of shooting him on the floor you have to climb hard and fast for your one shot and are not likely to get another. This lot led us a rare dance up the ridge and finally took off with their number still complete.

The Kirghiz came down that evening, looking a little wan but otherwise well. Gyalgen informed us that he had taken an even graver view of his own condition than we had, for after we had left him in the tent he had occupied himself drawing up his will. The feeling of remorse we experienced upon hearing this pathetic tale almost extinguished the disappointment to which his failure had contributed. But that evening the weather broke, much snow fell in the night, so after all we might not have got up Chakar Aghil.

Thus disappointed of our peak we indulged in a little mild exploration by returning over a new route. The local 'bojang', having now heard of our presence, carried us off to his yorts further up the At Oinak where he gave us a meal and also guides and ponies for the crossing of the Bostan Arche pass. The head of this glacier valley is enclosed by the western end of the cirque and the 20,500 ft. peak of Kara Boktor which is one of its two bastions. North of this peak the ridge droops and dwindles until it is easily crossed by the 13,000 ft. pass. Having topped this and taken our inevitable snack at a yort on the far side, we rode down a pleasant wooded valley to Yelche Moinak. But the pleasantness of these mountain valleys does not extend far down. Very soon the grass and the pines give way to bald, parched, eroded hills, the river as if in disgust buries itself in the gravel, and instead of kindly Kirghiz spacious in the possession of yaks, we find a few miserable bastard Kirghiz, gipsies rather than true nomads, with herds of goats which thrive in the wilderness they have helped to make.

At Yelche Moinak we joined the route by which we had descended in such crippled fashion from the Ulugh Art pass in 1947,[*] and two longish rides brought us back to Kashgar. I see that on the last day we covered the thirty-three miles to Kashgar in five hours, so that either I rode, as J.J. would say, uncommon galvanizingly, or else I drew a better mount than usually fell to my lot.

Owing to the impending departure of the twin pillars of Kashgar society, the British and Russian consuls, an epidemic of dining broke out. As rulers of Sinkiang the Chinese may not have deliberately set

---

[*] Crossing the Ulugh Art in 1947 Shipton's horse died, Mrs Shipton's was weary unto death, and the hired baggage ponies deserted. Three starving donkeys formed our train.

(56) The Geometry Peak of 'perpendicular faces and right-angled cut-offs'; It has nothing to do with the story, but 'when they bring you the heifer be ready with the rope'; in other words, if by some freak of fortune a good photograph turns up it should be used

(57) 'Our ridge overhung a broad snow plateau... Many thousands
of feet below lay the Oitagh valley, still in cold shadow'; the line of
cleavage of a pretty big avalanche can be seen in the cwm between
the ridge where we were standing and the snow plateau

themselves the task—the proper duty of a Colonial power—of making two blades of grass grow in place of one, but they have at least encouraged agriculture by consuming large quantities of produce. The Foreign Secretary struck first, and at his banquet, as was most fitting, the lion and the bear grazed amicably side by side. Glorious as they may be in feasting, the Chinese, as I have hinted, are not backward in drinking. The way in which successive bumpers (of a pitiless size) were downed on this occasion did something to restore one's confidence in the human race, but even so the pace was not hot enough for our mild-mannered host who introduced various quickening devices.

One of these was almost too simple for a sober man to appreciate but fortunately there was not one present. It consisted in the rapid circulation of a flow of match-boxes with a lighted match stuck in them and whosoever held the box when the match expired had to drain his glass. Provided the guests entered into the spirit of the thing a match could be made to expire in the hands of any half-hearted drinker with gratifying frequency. A noisier, more intellectual, and more effective method—for everyone might take part at once—was the stone, scissors, paper game, in which the opponents fling out their hands simultaneously to express one of the three symbols, the winner either wrapping up his opponent's stone, blunting his scissors, or cutting his paper. It is easy to play and not really necessary to explain. Even more noisy was the game in which the players in quick succession extend a certain number of fingers and guess at the combined total. It is no game for the inexperienced if the penalty exacted by the man who guesses right is the drinking of a glass of rice brandy. I had last seen this played in Italy (without the brandy) where the partisans took particular pleasure in it because Mussolini had formally banned the playing of it in albergos and other places where they sing. They played it with enormous speed and gusto, banging the knuckles hard on the table and shouting each time they showed their hands, which was just about as fast as one could count. After a long session the knuckles of the players hands would be bruised and swollen.

The dinner given by the G.O.C. Kashgar was a remarkably good one thanks to the absence of anything found in the sea and, in my opinion, mistakenly removed from it by the Chinese. One could therefore deal more or less faithfully with each dish on its merits, secure in the knowledge that no sea-slugs, shark-fin, traveller fish tripe, or seaweed soup, lurked obscenely in the bowl. One of the first-named I still carry about as a charm against bee stings or sea sickness until an opportunity occurs for planting it for the benefit of some geological friend in search of a trilobite which it much resembles. Departure from established custom, as our host regretfully explained, was owing to a recent memorandum circulated by the Central Government who, taking a leaf from the book of our own mandarins, severely discouraged luxury in high places. The curious ideas held by the Chinese on what constitutes 'food' naturally does nothing to limit their ideas when dealing with more ordinary fare. On this occasion we had, for example, ox-tail soup served in a half-melon, fried meat with cheese, and stewed pears stuffed with rice.

The Foreign Office and the Army having done their worst, we had little to fear from the Law, Civil Administration, Public Works, or even the Post Office. But by the time the epidemic had run its course the loess haze had, as it were, settled upon our complexions. 'You see', as the eminent Dr Swizzle used to say, 'it's all done by eating. Most people dig their grave with their teeth.' However, on the march home on which I had now to start there was to be little opportunity for that.

CHAPTER IX

TO MISGAR

———◆———

B Y THE END OF SEPTEMBER it was clear that as the incoming Indian consul would not soon arrive Shipton would have to leave before adjudicating upon the division of Chini Bagh into two equal halves for the respective Consulates of India and Pakistan—a delicate task which might well have baffled Solomon. He decided to delay his departure until mid-October and to proceed to India as quickly as possible. I, on the other hand, wanted leisure to deviate slightly from the direct route and so left ten days in advance. We expected to meet at Chitral. I have a rooted objection to following the beaten track, but because my deviations of the previous year had led me into trouble, this year I intended waiting until I was on the Indian side of the Mintaka pass before making any wide cast. Owing to the Kashmir dispute, the route which I should have liked to have taken was not possible.

In the absence of anyone in Kashgar anxious to see the world, and having no follower of my own, I arranged to travel with the mail runners. For the five-day stage to Tashkurghan the mails are carried on the ponies whose paces I had already tried and found wanting; but our friend Hill Billy, the Hunza lad, whose turn it was to go this trip, undertook to see me well mounted.

We had forty-three miles to do the first day to Yangi Hissar, so at the morbid hour of 2 a.m. I crept out of the Consulate to be hoisted with my two ruck-sacks and a bag of fodder on what might have been for all I knew a camel. I soon discovered that travelling with the mail was to be no picnic for I sat shivering in shorts and 'chapan', balanced high on the load with my legs dangling free, high on the beast's shoulder. The succeeding six hours of jogging and walking would have been unbroken had not my horse stumbled in the dark and saved me the trouble of dismounting by pitching me off. Breakfast-time had long passed when presently we turned in to a wayside house, dismounted

153

stiffly, and without staying to count the cost treated ourselves to a mealie cob—one each, that is to say.

Hill Billy's companion, evidently the senior of the half-section, was a little wizened, greybearded man—a Wakhi, I think—whose meagre frame was eminently in keeping with a ration of one mealie cob and whose stern ascetic expression hinted that no one should want or expect more. As for the horses they knew better than even to look as though they knew what food was. Since our stomachs would have regarded any long pause for digestion as derisory, we soon climbed on and took the road. When accomplishing this ungraceful act I was always reminded of the withering scorn with which the commander of a Horse Artillery battery, dissatisfied with their drill, instead of giving the order 'Mount', adjured his drivers to 'Climb up you ruddy monkeys'. In the absence of anyone to give him a friendly hoist, the would-be rider manoeuvres the beast alongside some bank or boulder and jumps for it, hoping the animal will be in the same place when he comes down.

We went on without a stop for another six hours to reach Yangi Hissar about four o'clock. The country was flat, sometimes with rich fields sometimes with wilderness, but on our right hand, austerely aloof, the Kungur range shone clearly. Seeing that their subsistence, their very being, is bound up with these mountains it is surprising how successfully the Turkis ignore them. I never saw them bestow even a passing glance upon these sources of life-giving water, much less go down upon their knees in the fields glorifying and prais-ing them. For all they cared the eternal snows might have been the Corporation reservoir. I like to think that even in these enlightened days our farmers remove their hats in reverence to welcome a timely shower of rain.

With knees permanently bent after the excruciating ride and wearing an old 'chapan' and a Hunza cap, I might have passed for one of the last survivors of Kolchak's White Russians had not Hill Billy disclosed his patron's high standing. The Chinese Amban invited me to stay the night, but pleading the necessity for an early start I put myself in the safer hands of the Aqsaqal, the local representative of the Indian trading community. Having eaten only the mealie cob since two o'clock that morning my thoughts were running on pilau,

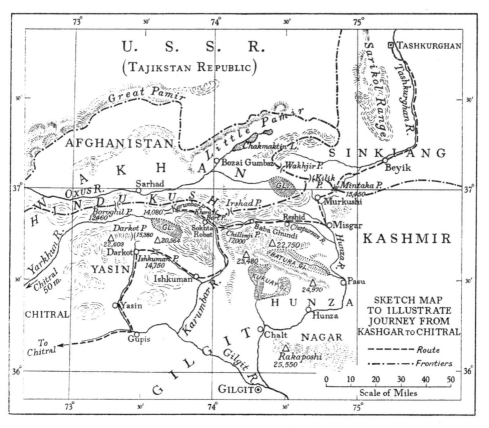

Map 4: Kashgar to Chitral

preferably the kind of Turkish pilau cooked by the great chef Alexis Soyer in the Crimea for 100 men, the recipe for which begins 'cut or chop 50 lb. of fresh mutton'. In due time an adequate meal was served. I should have preferred to have been quite alone to give it my undivided attention, for the Aqsaqal was too loquacious—ignorant, apparently, of the old Ruritanian proverb that every time the sheep bleats it loses a mouthful.

Our destination for the second stage was Aqsala, the road still running south skirting the foothills. We left at 5 a.m. fresh and fasting, halted for an inexpensive mealie cob lunch at Igiz Yar, the last oasis of the Kashgarian plain, and stopped for the night in a serai some miles short of our destination. The serai was run by a Turki woman, a little tawny but quite comely, and bearing in mind the adage, 'the fairer the hostess the fouler the reckoning', I was surprised we stopped at either this or any other inn because my couriers seemed to have friends to greet or business to transact at almost every house. We had now turned eastwards heading for the mountains up a valley in which next morning we rode in shadow until after ten o'clock. Even the greybearded Wakhi, who disliked walking, had to get off occasionally to keep warm (59). Now that we had passed beyond cultivation there was no point in dismounting in search of mealie cobs, we therefore carried on without food or drink until we halted for the night at a couple of yorts. I did not mind this, for I should hardly regard a mealie cob as an adequate reason for getting off a bicycle let alone a horse, and when riding there is really no need for food, at least not for the rider.

In this narrow sunless valley my two stalwarts found it too cold even for them to make an early start. We had some lost ground to make up if we were to reach Tashkurghan next day, but after a late start and with two passes to cross there seemed little chance of doing so. Although it was already late when we dropped down from the Tari Art (13,340 ft.) to the Karatash valley at Toilebelung, where there was a serai and a Chinese post, we did not stop. Scorning the serai and grimacing at the soldiers we entered the mouth of the Tangitar gorge in which just before dark we were received at a miserable hovel with a hearty welcome. Without counting dogs, calves, and lambs, there were already fifteen inside so three more made little difference. The women added a little more water to an already watery stew, Hill Billy

(58) This picture of Muztagh Ata (24,388 ft.) was taken the previous
year (1947) from the roof of the fort at Subashi west of the mountain;
the summit is in cloud and the ridge which took us very nearly but
not quite there is the right-hand skyline

(59) Hill Billy's wizened comrade (centre) invited me to get off and
look at this hunting eagle which was being carried to Kashgar; it is
lashed to the back of a donkey, only the head, feet, and tail being visible; these eagles are trained to hunt small antelope, foxes, and even
wolves; Skrine in *Chinese Central Asia* describes a similar black eagle
which measured 3 ft. from beak to tail, with a wing-spread of 7 ft.;
dull black with a ruff of rust-coloured feathers, yellow claws, black
beak with yellow base, and red-brown eyes; the mounted sportsman
carries the bird like a hawk on his wrist which has to be supported by
a wooden prop from the saddle

disclosed a hidden reserve of mealie cobs, and I contributed a cigarette. Nearly all fifteen, including the children, had a pull at it and all
were extremely grateful.

When we started not very early on the fifth day I hardly expected
that we should reach Tashkurghan for it was still nearly forty miles
away on the other side of the Chichiklik pass (15,400 ft.). For several
miles the boulders in the river-bed of the gorge, which was, of course,
the track, kept the ponies to a walk. Soon after midday we emerged
upon the great grass plateau, the Chichiklik maidan, and bumped
across it at a good pace in the teeth of a shrivelling blast—a feature of
this region upon which many travellers from Hsuan Tsang (A.D. 624)
downwards have remarked. In 1947, a month earlier, we had crossed
it one dull evening with snow on the ground when there was slightly
less cold than we now experienced at midday under a brilliant sun.
Beyond the maidan the road climbs gently to the pass and then drops
rapidly for 5000 ft. through a cruel gorge strewn with the skeletons
and mummified bodies of donkeys. A dead donkey is a forlorn object
but one which his living brother very sensibly, I suppose, meets with
indifference. Nevertheless, I personally felt that this goodly fellowship
of death would have looked better had the skeletons of one or two of
their owners been stretched alongside their animals.

Once we had quitted this horrible nallah we had good going
upon which the tireless beasts jogged rapidly towards the green Tagharma vale, while away to the north the mighty dome of Muztagh Ata
(58) flushed in the setting sun. At length, as darkness fell, we reached
the poplars and the stone tower of Tashkurghan, the empty bazaar
and the deserted serais of this seedy capital of Sarikol. I reckoned
that in five days the horses had covered about 150 miles, carrying a
man as well as a load, on a ration which can safely be described as
meagre. In the strength of horses such as this the psalmist might well
have taken pleasure.

It is all very well to speak of the capital of Sarikol, but one must
not expect too much from a village 10,000 ft. up, which happens to
be the largest one in a poor, straggling, inclement district. No part
of Sarikol is lower than this, and most of it is much higher, com-
prising as it does the eastern edge of the Pamirs, the valley of the
Tashkurghan river and the Tagharma valley, both of which descend

to Tashkurghan. Kirghiz inhabit the Pamirs and Tajiks the valleys, where they grow barley. It is a place of great antiquity, but one suspects that even the ancients, superior as they no doubt were to their descendants, could have done little with such a place. Anyhow no trace remains of the stupa built, according to the Chinese pilgrim Hsuan Tsang, by Asoka (264 B.C.), nor of the convent built in honour of a Buddhist monk of Taxila in the Punjab who preached to the Sarikolis. Neither does Marco Polo tell us anything of what it was like in his day (c. 1270), for he leaps in his headlong way from the upper Oxus to Kashgar in what he calls 'forty good days', pausing only to revile the idolaters met with on the way who were 'in truth an evil race'. Even Col. Yule, Marco's thorough and pious editor, who has elucidated much, can add nothing to this, nor tell us whether or not Marco passed through Tashkurghan. It is very rare, but it happens occasionally, that a traveller's tale is too succinct.

From Tashkurghan to Misgar on the Indian side of the Mintaka pass the mail bags are carried on donkeys, one of which I hired for my kit. After a day's rest Hill Billy and the ponies started back for Kashgar, and our party of three donkeys, two Hunza men, and myself headed south. Certainly, as the ponies stepped proudly out of the gate and we shambled after them I felt I had taken a step down in the world, but from Misgar onwards I should have to fall lower and begin carrying a load myself. Just before we left my rage had kindled against these two donkey drivers by reason of their refusal to accept payment for my donkey in Sinkiang dollars, and since the number of rupees offered for them by the Shylocks of the bazaar was quite ridiculous I ceremonially burnt the ten million I had left—a haughty gesture which fell disappointingly flat.

The two stages to Dafdar, thirty-four miles away, are not kind to the man on foot; whichever side of the river is taken, the way lies over a featureless gravel plain. When going southwards the traveller has not even the inspiration of the kingly Muztagh Ata to which to lift his eyes for now it lies directly behind him. Beyond Dafdar the man on foot may take heart, he has done with deserts and gravel plains and is entering the region where, if he has good lungs, he is on more than equal terms with a horse. After crossing the Oprang river, which was not now the obstacle it is in high summer, the Taghdumbash Pamir

closes in upon the valley, and a river of clear cobalt blue, dashing over
a white pebble bed, becomes an intimate and cheerful companion by
the roadway. I noticed that the number of Kirghiz yorts had greatly
increased since I passed this way in 1947; then there had been only a
few clustered round Beyik, but now there were many on both banks of
the river. No doubt they belonged to some of the thirty families whose
vanguard I had met in 1947 crossing the Wakhjir pass.

At Mintaka Karaul, beyond Beyik, I met the chief of these people
living, as befitted him, in the most princely and spacious yort I had yet
seen. The rugs, the highly ornamented saddlery, and the pile of brightly
coloured boxes against the wall, testified that the owner was a man of
substance. He was very friendly and very well-informed. He had heard
of and regretted the departure of the British Consul from Kashgar,
and he spat at the mention of the Russians who were apparently the
reason for the migration of his tribe from their grazing grounds near
the Chakmaktin lake in Wakhan. Although he spoke no English he
could read the names of places on my map, and seemingly was familiar
with all the country from Wakhan to the Murghab. He was eager to
talk; but, naturally, he understood quite as well as I did that an empty
stomach has no ears. When his women had placed in front of me a
large wooden bowl of thick cream and a suitable acreage of flat, fresh
loaves, I gave him what attention I could spare.

On 11 October we started early from a yort at Lupgaz which is the
last habitation on the Chinese side of the Mintaka pass. No doubt we
should have fared better at the chief's yort, but our resting places were
usually dictated by the necessities of trade of which the mail couriers privately did a good deal, picking up wool, skins, and numdahs
at all kinds of out-of-the-way places. The unfortunate donkeys' loads
had increased, were increasing, and no doubt ought to have been
diminished, but the only diminution was in their pace. I welcomed
this because, though I generally dislike donkeys as baggage animals
on account of their despicably slow pace, up to Beyik it had been as
much as I could do to keep up with our three flyers. Donkey driving
is an art in which a stout cudgel and a strong arm are of less avail than
knowledge of the appropriate cries and the skill to utter them. Stevenson found that the application of a wand with an eighth of an inch
of pin to Modestine's mousey-coloured rump had a very galvanising

effect, and the fat Turki, sitting astride his donkey, indifferently uses the point of his knife.

Just beyond Lupgaz we found the unwelcome innovation of a Chinese check post where they turned all my kit on to the road. No one, least of all the Chinese soldiers, knew what they were looking for, but the search occupied one of their many idle hours and gave them a lot of fun. Apart from the inconvenience, it is humiliating to have one's belongings exposed to public view on an Asiatic highway, where the contents of even a rucksack must look shamefully superfluous in the eyes of men who travel further and no less comfortably with nothing whatever. It is impossible, we are told, to do any act not in itself morally wrong for the last time without feelings of regret. There may have been a slight moral taint about my last dealings with Chinese soldiers and customs officials—for I had in my pocket a piece of jade which I intended keeping there—but I experienced slight regret and certainly no remorse as I looked upon them for probably the last time. Their presence accorded ill with my notion of the fitness of things. In this bleak but noble landscape with which the Kirghiz and his yaks were quite in harmony, the occupants of this post—disreputable and slightly insolent—struck a jarring note. Since mountain ranges are so often frontiers it is unreasonable, I suppose, to expect that the passes should not be guarded, but along the frontiers of the Himalaya and the Hindu Kush it is only people like the Chinese and the Afghans who have the childish notion that the only way to guard a pass is to sit upon it. Whatever goes up into the mountains must soon come down, so that it is sensible, cheaper, and more agreeable to the parties concerned, if the frontier guards wait at the bottom for this to happen, leaving the mountains themselves free of their discordant presence so that the felicity of mountaineers and travellers may be more perfect.

In shorts and shirt-sleeves, for it was a calm sunny day, and rejoicing to think that on the far side there were neither soldiers nor officials, I continued the way to the Mintaka pass (15,450 ft.) (60, 61). The delay occasioned by this kit inspection could not be made up by rattling down the other side, for baggage animals, particularly donkeys, pick their way down with cautious, stilted steps, at even slower pace than they go up. At the foot of the Mintaka pass there are some rather snug caves occupied in summer by goatherds. They had gone down by now,

(60) The approach to the Mintaka pass from the Sinkiang side is up
a typical Pamir valley with wide, flat, slightly swampy bottom; the
pass (15,450 ft.) is the lowest point on the ridge immediately above
the leading donkey

(61) The country on the Pakistan side of the Mintaka pass is very different—a typical Himalayan glacier, boulder strewn, flanked by rock walls, and fed by tributary ice-falls; the peak (*c.* 21,000 ft.) is the westernmost bastion of the Karakoram range; further west the watershed and the frontier are formed by the Hindu Kush

but I went to the caves where I lit a fire assuming we should stop there, but the donkeys held resolutely on their way to Murkushi which we reached long after dark. It is a place well suited to benighted travellers. Water is hard by and fuel even nearer to hand, for the camp is pitched upon a thick seam of dry goat dung, the deposit of ages. It can be dug up in bricks like peat. But it is an even better fuel, and burns with hardly any smoke.

When we reached Misgar next day it was time for me to quit the beaten track which I had followed quite far enough. Misgar, at the end of a telegraph line, is ten stages from Gilgit, whence roads go either to Abbottabad by the Babusar pass and Kagan valley (about fifteen days), or to Chitral in about ten days. Instead of going to Chitral by Gilgit it would be a little shorter in theory and in practice certainly much more amusing to strike across country by way of the Chapursan nallah, the Chillinji pass (17,000 ft.), the Karumbar pass, and thence by the Yarkhun valley to Chitral. This route, which follows pretty closely the south side of the Hindu Kush, would be of particular interest for me because in the previous year we had intended to traverse a part of it but had failed.

The Hunza men of Misgar professed ignorance of the route, but provided a man and a donkey to come with me as far as Reshid, the principal village of the Chapursan valley where I was assured I should find a guide. This assurance was hardly justified. When we reached Reshid I had to draw many maps in the dust of the headman's veranda, where I had settled for the night, before he had even an inkling of what I wanted to do. At last one or two of the audience of the pavement artists' graphic work grasped the key to these problem pictures and began bawling out the names of places on the itinerary, very few of which figured on my map. However, the headman promised that two volunteers, or, if necessary, conscripts would be found, meantime I might go on to the head of the valley with a pony and await the event at the local Mecca, the tomb of Baba Ghundi.

CHAPTER X

TO CHITRAL

T HE CHAPURSAN IS A FINE OPEN VALLEY inhabited by Wakhis from
Wakhan. Despite the great elevation of over 10,000 ft., they grow
wheat, any surplus being taken by Kirghiz who reach the valley from
Wakhan by the Irshad pass (16,060 ft.). The floor of the valley is flat
and easily irrigated, but a hundred years ago much of it was devastated
by a great flood which covered the fertile land with a thick deposit of
clay and boulders. Above Reshid the valley is still littered with high
mounds of this stuff like great ant-heaps. The flood was presumably
caused by the formation of a glacier dam like that which dammed the
Shyok river in 1929 when a lake 1000 yd. broad and 25 ft. deep accu-
mulated. This burst on the morning of 15 August, with a noise 'like a
cannon-shot'. Two days later at Patab Pul, the bridge below the great
'knee-bend' of the Indus 300 miles away, the river rose 45 ft. Loss of
life and damage to property were remarkably little.

At Yashkuk, where we had to ford the deep stream of the Yashkuk
glacier, there is a pleasant oasis of grass and thorn trees. We met there
a company of some twenty pilgrims, men, women, and children, who
had been to pay their respects at the shrine of Baba Ghundi (62). The
tradition is that when this prophet found, as is customary, that he was
without honour in his own country, he took a short way with dissenters
by wiping out the whole valley with the aid of this memorable flood,
an apostolic knock which earned him implicit respect and obedience
for the rest of his life and utmost veneration after his death. Pilgrims
from Wakhan and even Gilgit visit the shrine, and the Mir of Hunza,
who has a rest-house hard by, takes a personal interest in its upkeep.

The shrine itself, which, according to Schomberg,[*] does not con-
tain the saint's remains, is a small tomb of mud and stone covered with
a wooden roof, enclosed by a high stone wall. At a gate in the wall is

---

[*]   R. C. F. Schomberg, *Between Oxus and Indus.*

(62) Inside the modern stone wall, built by the Mir of Hunza, is an old mud and stone wall and the shrine of Baba Ghundi surrounded by fluttering flags; according to Schomberg (*Between Oxus and Indus*) the shrine is merely a cenotaph marking the place where the saint, having driven home his convincing theological argument, vanished from human sight

(63) Koz Yaz glacier descending from the Kukuay-Batura watershed;
in 1947 we had hoped to cross this range at the head of the glacier,
but there is obviously no way down this side unless there is one out
of sight round the corner to left or right

a huge pile of old ibex horns and within is a perfect forest of poles adorned with white flags and yaks' tails, the offerings of pilgrims. The caretaker of the shrine also looks after some of the Mir's more worldly interests in the form of a herd of yaks and a flock of sheep. Some barley is grown, and this, when I was there, was being removed from holes in the ground and spread out to dry.

I began to think I might have to return to Reshid, having been pushed off here perhaps by the headman merely for the sake of peace and quiet, so I kept the pony until next morning when at ten o'clock the chosen victims arrived, clamouring for bread. Grudgingly I doled out some atta, having brought with me only 30 lb. which would have to do for the three of us until we reached the first habitations in the Yarkhun valley. Besides this I had some tea and sugar but nothing else, not even a tent or a Primus stove. The Wakhis having fed and invoked the protection of the saint, we shouldered our burdens, crossed the river, and proceeded up the north bank accompanied by two mounted Kirghiz. These had spent the night at Baba Ghundi in religious meditation alleviated by opium, and at the Irshad nallah, a few miles up, they turned off for the pass to Wakhan. I sent with them my respects to 'Father', the Kirghiz chief on the other side, who in 1947 had prevented me from crossing back into India by that pass. Indeed this upper Chapursan had other objects of wistful interest for me. We passed on the south side the white rampart of the Kukuay-Batura watershed, and the Yashkuk and Koz Yaz (63) glaciers descending from it, down either of which we should, in 1947, have been delighted to come had the topography only accorded more with our ideas and less with reality.

The red rock conglomerate walls of the valley drew together for a brief space into a gorge to open out again upon the grass and boulder covered moraine of the Chillinji glacier. Here, at a spot known as Buattar (64), is a sheepfold and a cave under a great rock in which we spent the night.

According to my altimeter which registered only 13,000 ft. we were faced with a longish climb to the pass. My two heroes seemed aware of this, but by no means dismayed; indeed, they talked boldly of reaching Sokhta Robat several miles up the Karumbar valley on the other side of the pass. Accordingly we broke camp at 2 a.m. A waning moon shed enough light to have shown us the path had there been one, but the men seemed to know very well what they were about. Instead of making for the glacier they struck straight up the hillside by a route which presently became a rock-climb. At first light we began a downward traverse to the glacier, now some way below and just beginning to emerge from the uncertain gloom; and when the first rays of the sun struck fire from tall peaks guarding the pass the glacier still lay cold and grey, the ice of its surface-water crackling underfoot.

The easy slope of névé upon which we presently embarked looked so short that I allowed but half an hour for the ascent; but two hours later the rigidly distant snow horizon still mocked my longing eyes. Far behind were the two black specks of my companions, whose eyes, I imagined, would be fixed on the same goal with less longing and some despair. Though they were not carrying much more and had also the benefit of my laborious track, they made heavy weather of it. They were suffering in milder form the pangs of the cadaverous Kirghiz on Chakar Aghil and with no more reason, for they too had lived all their lives at over 10,000 ft. This not only puzzled but grieved me because I had counted on them to break a trail for my own wavering steps. It was even more puzzling to find that there should be any need for breaking a trail after a cold night in the middle of October and after a long spell of fine sunny weather.

Alas! the fine spell of weather had ended. As I topped the last rise I was greeted by a cold wind driving before it menacing clouds which already hung low upon the tangle of peaks to the west of the Karumbar valley (65). The rising wind cutting short the lamentations of my men, addressed principally to me as the author of their misery, we hastened down 6000 ft. of scree slopes to whatever shelter the Karumbar valley might afford. We made for a nallah on our right which appeared the easiest approach to the main valley. It was an unhappy choice, there was no hint of a path amongst the boulders and birch scrub of the stream bed along which we had to fight a way for the best part of an hour. At last we emerged on to a sandy flat in the main valley where I was pleased to find a very faintly marked track and a cave. It was raining by now. There was no longer any talk of Sokhta Robat, indeed from the 'misere' sung by the two Wakhis I gathered that if ever they left the cave it would be to go down the Karumbar valley and not up.

(64) Beyond the black gorge lies the sheepfold of Buattar from where
we started for the Chillinji pass which is out of sight to the left;
according to Schomberg, 'buatta' is the name of a plant whose root
is a powerful purgative

(65) The country immediately west of the Chillinji presents a wild
tangle of peaks and valleys and is very vaguely surveyed; most of the
peaks in sight look eminently unclimbable

The one whose headache was least severe began searching for a flat stone upon which he mixed into a dough and shaped into the semblance of a thick chapattie the flour I gave him. Upon this we dined, reserving a little of the bread for breakfast, and after they had made a second brew of tea from my used tea leaves I gave them a cigarette. This cheered them up, and I enlarged upon the number of rupees they would have earned by the time we reached Chitral. They now confessed that they had never been beyond this point, but they agreed to go on until we came upon some habitation. They would then be free to return. Money is the only argument such men understand. I had not seen much of Wakhis, but I soon realized that nothing could be got by appealing to that which they did not have—a liking for mild adventure, curiosity to see what was in the next valley, or shame at the thought of turning back.

When we woke to a dull, windy morning we saw that new snow had fallen down to about 14,000 ft. Having forded the river we picked up a faint track which we followed for five miles of good, flat going to Sokhta Robat which is a name and nothing more. A little grass, dwarf willow and silver birch, and the fire-blackened stones of someone's camp, alone marked the spot. Across the river a fairly well-defined track zigzagged up steep slopes to the Khora Bort, another pass into Wakhan. Our track hugged the south side of the valley until we lost it in an ablation valley between the valley wall and a high moraine from which we looked down upon the Chashboi glacier. The Karumbar valley has no glacier of its own, but at this point it is completely filled by the ice of the Chashboi, which emerges from a comparatively short and narrow lateral valley, spreads like spilt tar over the wide floor of the Karumbar, laps up against the opposing north wall, and then turns and flows grandly down the valley to the east (66). The mountain which produces all this ice must be well worth looking at, unluckily the weather was now so thick that we never saw it.

The glacier had to be crossed, so we dropped down into the trough where on a patch of mud I picked up the tracks of a pony and then lost them. The Wakhis were not good trackers, so I threaded a way through the stony labyrinth on the flank of the glacier and launched boldly out on to the smoother ice surface beyond. By reason of its size and its crevasses the Chashboi is a very considerable obstacle, and although I had proof that ponies had been taken across it I was glad we were not so encumbered. It was enough to have two half-willing Wakhis who, like most natives of the Himalaya (Sherpas are an exception), have a singular distaste for walking over ice or snow—a reluctance which is not wholly accounted for by their usually dilapidated footwear. My two men were no worse off in this respect than most, and each had with him a few square inches of goatskin with which in the evening he made good the losses of the day. They were the usual high, soft-skinned boots which are not much good for anything except riding. It is singular that I have never seen anyone wearing a new pair of these boots, just as one seldom sees a man with a new pair of homespun trousers or a coat. The women still weave cloth, but some curious economic law, similar perhaps to that which prevails nearer home, denies their menfolk the benefit of their industry.

We spent two hours on the ice before putting this great barrier behind us—an obstacle, which, I hoped, would make the Wakhis think twice before turning back. Before us lay a broad, upland valley with nothing but the 14,000 ft. Karumbar pass at its head. Towards evening a drizzling rain set in which made us careful in the selection of a rock by which to sleep. Eventually we found one which after a little digging with the ice-axe afforded some protection. The height was about 12,500 ft. and from my map, which was on a scale of only sixteen miles to the inch, I thought we must be six or seven miles from the pass.

In the night the rain turned to snow which, eddying around our rock, covered us all as with a shroud. This, I thought, will finish it. Nevertheless, we coaxed a fire of sorts with the wet heath, ate the remains of last night's bread, and started. On the north side of the valley, to which we had now crossed, we picked up a track which, thanks to the three or four inches of new snow, stood out clearly. Nothing showed at one's feet, but by looking well ahead the faint trace became visible. This discovery had a very heartening effect on all; for though a contempt for tracks is to be encouraged as a sign of an independent mind there are times when such independence proves very expensive. I was no less relieved than the Wakhis; by now the valley had become so wide as to be an open moor where mist and sleet extinguished all landmarks.

But as we slowly gained height the snow increased in depth until it was kneedeep. This not only made walking difficult, but quite

(66) A couple of miles above Sokhta Robat the wide flat floor of the
Karumbar valley is completely blocked by the great ice stream of the
Chashboi; this glacier descends from a short side valley to the south
and flows across to the rock wall by which it is deflected down the
Karumbar; the mountain wall on the right is part of the Hindu Kush
and the Wakhan frontier, but the range is losing height here and can
be crossed some ten miles further west by the comparatively low
(12,000 ft.) Boroghil pass

(67) Although this is fairly low down and despite the presence here
of an ass, a cow, and a few dwarf willows, the Karumbar valley is still
a savage place; here an old terminal moraine nearly blocks the valley
(the main river is to the right of the bushes), and from the deep-cut
valleys beyond two more glaciers will thrust almost to the river

obliterated the friendly trace. In these new conditions the Wakhi's morale, which had never been high, sank at once. Upon this trackless waste of snow, cut by a shrewd wind, they sat down and wept; 'We shall all die', was the burthen of their lament. Our case was not quite as bad as that; with a couple of Sherpas one might have struggled on or waited for better weather, but with these men there was nothing to be done. I made several wide casts in the hope of recovering the track and when these failed the Wakhis insisted on retreat. Bowing to fate, an act of homage to which I was now accustomed, I gave the word.

Before recrossing the Chashboi, which we reached that same evening, we picked up a line of guiding marks. They were not quite cairns, but to practised eyes a couple of stones or even a single stone placed on a boulder are sufficient indication. Following these up we took to the ice at what must be the usual crossing place. Since the ice-crossing was shorter, this may be the best route for ponies, but it landed us too soon in the trough on the other side for we had to make a very rough passage down it. Next morning as we were approaching the big bend near the Chillinji caves we fell in with a party of Kirghiz and four yaks. They had crossed the Khora Bort the previous day and were on their way down the Karumbar to Ishkuman to barter butter and wool for grain.

Instead of recrossing the Chillinji pass my best way now was down to Ishkuman whither the Wakhis consented to come. The path down the Karumbar nallah (67) is one of the roughest and most difficult of these parts and is little used; in summer, owing to the unfordable river and the steepness of the rock walls, it is virtually impassable. Thirty years ago no less than four glaciers, descending from the Kukuay watershed to the east, pushed their ice right down to the river, one of them, the Karumbar, abutting against the rocks on the west bank. In 1916 Dr Longstaff found the first of these, the Chillinji, and the second below it, the Wargot, just touching the water; in 1905 the Wargot is said to have formed a dam which, when it broke, caused flooding as far down the river as Gilgit. When we passed, both these glaciers stopped well short of the water, while the Karumbar, under which in 1916 the river had tunnelled a way, now stopped short by a hundred yards.

We spent the night at a place called Buk Buk where there were a hut, a field, and two Wakhis. Judging by the expression of consternation on the faces of these two, the story to which they were now compelled to listen lost nothing in the telling. A survivor of the retreat from Moscow could hardly have made more of the length of the way, the depth of the snow, and the severity of the weather. To hear these Wakhis talking one might think they had no teeth, but I discovered that it was the curious effect of talking with a quid of tobacco in either cheek. The linguist of my party, that is the one who spoke a little Hindustani, usually tried to be rude to me, in which, with his mouth full of tobacco, he usually succeeded. I never much cared for either of them but as porters their one great point was that they carried nothing whatever of their own.

In the rather forlorn hope of reaching Imit, the chief village and the residence of the rajah of Ishkuman, we started very early next morning. Before sun-up we had had to ford the main river twice as well as a small but fast side stream. The last crossing of the main river was so long and deep that by the time I crawled out I was almost whimpering with cold. Below Bhort, where there was an interesting looking glacier, the track improved, but we did not reach Imit until next morning. The rajah, who had already heard of our arrival in his valley, sent one of his brothers to escort me in. The brothers of the rajahs of the Gilgit Agency, who are, of course, much more numerous than the rajahs themselves, have always been a difficulty. According to one's point of view, a ruling caste which cannot find jobs for its male relatives is no less worthy of sympathy than a government which cannot find jobs for the boys. Without land of his own to make or mar, the only other opening in these parts for a member of this caste— a 'gushpur'—is polo; this is proper enough, for it is a manly occupation and one which unlike many others does not interfere with other people's business. But with the best will in the world it cannot be made an all-time job.

I enjoyed a day's rest as a guest of the rajah. He did not know me, and my travel-stained appearance can hardly have been a satisfactory introduction, but he made me welcome on the grounds that I was an Englishman. Whatever the British may have done or left undone in the past, it is something to know that in these remote regions an Englishman is sure to meet with a very warm welcome.

Hoping to save something from the wreck of my plan I decided that instead of following the valley down to Gilgit I would cross the Ishkuman pass to Darkot whence by going north over the Darkot pass

(68) The plain of Mastuj, seen here, is still three long marches from Chitral; it is on the Chitral-Gilgit road and the road to the Shandur pass and thence to Gilgit, by which I came, lies up the shadowed valley to the left; on top of the Shandur (*c.* 13,000 ft.) is the Chitral-Gilgit boundary, a lake stocked with trout, and a polo ground—three lasting tributes to British rule

(69) Journey's end; the bridge over the Yarkhun river and beyond it
the mosque, the Mehtar's palace, and the plane trees of Chitral

I might still reach the head of the Yarkhun valley. Much more snow than I expected had fallen on the Ishkuman pass (14,750 ft.), and since it was newly fallen winter snow it was powdery. In summer, I was told, a strong man could go to Darkot and back in a day; it took us two and a half days to get there, and at the end of the second day my three Ishkuman men were so exhausted that they would not even bestir themselves to make bread; an extraordinary state of languor which was perhaps more indicative of the badness of the coolies than that of the road.

Darkot village, 9000 ft. up, lies at the foot of the Darkot pass (15,380 ft.) to the north of which is Chitral. The pass lies on the southern and higher branch of the Hindu Kush, separated from the lower and altogether milder northern range by the valley of the Yarkhun. Close on either side of the Darkot rise peaks of 21,000 and 22,000 ft. whereas, some ten miles north, the main range can be crossed at just over 12,000 ft. by the Boroghil pass, within twenty miles of which there are no high mountains at all. A road for wheeled vehicles could be easily made over the Boroghil were there any place on either side of it to which a wheeled vehicle could profitably go.

Both these passes are interesting on account of the discoveries made by Sir Aurel Stein in connection with them. In A.D. 747 a Chinese general led a force of 10,000 men from Kashgar across the Pamirs to concentrate them at Sarahad on the Oxus on the Wakhan side of the Boroghil. His object was to oust the Tibetans who were threatening the Chinese hold on the Tarim basin (the 'Western Kingdoms') in conjunction with their allies, the Arabs, who were advancing up the Oxus valley. After carrying the positions held by the Tibetans defending the Boroghil the Chinese forced the pass, crossed the Darkot pass unopposed, and proceeded down the valley to Yasin and Gilgit. To this one can only add that the presence of a Tibetan army on the Boroghil was hardly less remarkable than the success of the Chinese in driving them off. I suppose it is no more strange than that Japanese should be found fighting in Burma or Germans in North Africa, but it is a striking commentary on the vicissitudes of nations and a queer illustration of geopolitics that Arabs and Tibetans in alliance should be at grips with Chinese upon the barren mountains of Wakhan.

With the experience of the Ishkuman pass fresh in my mind I decided that the Darkot pass, 1000 ft. higher, should not be attempted, and that I must at last resign myself to a more usual route. And I was the more resigned—in fact eager to do it—on account of a talk I had had with two traders from Gilgit who soon after our arrival had joined the throng of idlers and travellers in the headman's house. When I had left Kashgar the situation in Berlin had looked ticklish enough, so I was half prepared to believe these worthies when, after retailing the more important news of the bombing of Gilgit, they casually added that for the last ten days Pakistan, as they put it, with her allies Great Britain and America, was at war with Russia.

There was no time to be lost. Modern wars are such long drawn out affairs that it would not be easy to arrive too late to take part, yet it would never do to commit such a solecism. In a terrible stew, hot-foot and resolved to march double stages, I set out for Gupis and the beaten track which I could no longer shun (68). A day later, I learnt that a more or less deep peace still brooded over Europe, Africa, and Asia. In seven more days, on 4 November, I reached Chitral (69) thirty-five days out from Kashgar.

H. W. TILMAN

The Collected Edition

FOR THE FIRST TIME SINCE THEIR ORIGINAL APPEARANCE, all fifteen books by H. W. Tilman are being published as single volumes, with all their original photographs, maps and charts. Forewords and afterwords by those who knew him, or who can bring their own experience and knowledge to bear, complement his own understated writing to give us a fuller picture of the man and his achievements. A sixteenth volume is the 1980 biography by J. R. L. Anderson, *High Mountains and Cold Seas*. The books will appear in pairs, one each from his climbing and sailing eras, in order of original publication, at quarterly intervals from September 2015:

www.tilmanbooks.com